Corning Pyroceram® Cookware

Debbie and Randy Coe

Schiffer Publishing Ltd
4880 Lower Valley Road · Atglen, PA 19310

Schiffer Books are available at special discounts for bulk purchases for sales promotions or premiums. Special editions, including personalized covers, corporate imprints, and excerpts can be created in large quantities for special needs. For more information contact the publisher:

Published by Schiffer Publishing Ltd.
4880 Lower Valley Road
Atglen, PA 19310
Phone: (610) 593-1777; Fax: (610) 593-2002
E-mail: Info@schifferbooks.com

For the largest selection of fine reference books on this and related subjects, please visit our web site at **www.schifferbooks.com**
We are always looking for people to write books on new and related subjects. If you have an idea for a book please contact us at the above address.

This book may be purchased from the publisher.
Include $5.00 for shipping.
Please try your bookstore first.
You may write for a free catalog.

In Europe, Schiffer books are distributed by
Bushwood Books
6 Marksbury Ave.
Kew Gardens
Surrey TW9 4JF England
Phone: 44 (0) 20 8392-8585; Fax: 44 (0) 20 8392-9876
E-mail: info@bushwoodbooks.co.uk
Website: www.bushwoodbooks.co.uk
Free postage in the U.K., Europe; air mail at cost.

Library of Congress Control Number: 2008932958

Designed by RoS
Type set in Kabel BK BT/ Zurich BT

ISBN: 978-0-7643-3139-8
Printed in China

On title page:
Display of the patterns of: Blue Cornflower, Wildflower, Floral Bouquet, Forever Yours, Spice O' Life, Pastel Bouquet, Sears, Amana.

Contents

Dedication

We would like to dedicate this book to Donald Stookey, who was a true pioneer in glass research. His determination and curiosity to develop new products in the glass chemistry field led to the discovery of Pyroceram®, a wonderful substance that has glass-ceramic properties. Because of him, Corning Ware® came into existence and made the convenience of preparing a meal so much easier. We applaud his efforts.

Donald Stookey holding a Wildflower casserole. *Photo courtesy of American Ceramic Society and Donald Stookey.*

Acknowledgments

Compiling this book took a great many people to be generous with their glassware, knowledge, and time. They assisted in so many different ways by helping us find the pieces, providing glass and/ or catalogs for us to photograph, sharing their expertise, plus giving us leads to people to contact.

We are so grateful for the help from the following people: Jack Alleckson, Darlene & Gordon Cochran, Tom Dimitroff, Tom Felt, Amelia, Myra & Stephen Hixson, Debbie & Ed Lane, Tara & Jeff McRitchie, Mark Mecklenborg, Jaime Wilson, Peter Wray, and Jerry & Ginny Wright.

A huge thanks goes to Gail Bardhan, Reference and Research librarian from the Corning Museum of Glass Rakow Library. She was truly a big help making copies of catalogs for us and answering so many questions. She was also gracious enough to proof our material. Living on the west coast and not having easy access to the library was made so much easier by this wonderful lady. She was always available to give us assistance or find us answers.

Another huge amount of assistance was given by Kris Gable of the Corning Archives. She was a big help in locating information for us and proofing some of our material. She provided some much needed information.

Replacements founder and current CEO, Bob Page, along with his partner, Dale Fredrickson granted us permission to use the Corning pieces they have in their inventory. We greatly appreciate having access to these patterns to further enhance this book. Dean Six, a terrific friend, who is also a researcher at Replacements was instrumental in getting the information sent to us. Also out of his own collection, he shared archival material of the Corning factories. We appreciate his expertise at answering many of our odd inquiries.

We greatly appreciate the help that Karen Radcliff provided us by giving the correct translation on the French words that were on the Spice O' Life pieces.

We appreciate having access to the archival material at both the Corning Museum of Glass in Corning, New York, and West Virginia American Museum of Glass in Weston, West Virginia. These museums have spent so much time and money gathering together and then cataloging materials to have available to fellow researchers. These libraries were very instrumental in helping us complete this project

Lastly, we so treasure being able to have contact with Donald Stookey. He was terrific in supplying us additional information. If it wasn't for his expertise, the Corning cookware would not exist. His quest for new developments in glass, led to the discovery of Pyroceram®.

We applaud all of you for contributing to the success of this project!

Introduction

Corning brochure of Fry, Boil, Broil, Bake, Freeze and Serve all in the same dish. *Reprinted with permission from Corning Incorporated.*

We would like to celebrate the 50th anniversary of Corning cookware with the publication of this book in 2008. It is hard to believe that 50 years ago in 1958, Corning introduced the new Pyroceram® cookware that they called Corning Ware®. This was an extraordinary event that would have an impact on consumers for many years.

According to the *Gaffer News*, a publication of Corning Glass Works for their employees, it was announced that the new cookware was first revealed in a test marketing area of New England in August of 1958. One of the major stores, Shepard's, located in Providence, Rhode Island, reported excellent responses from customers, which resulted in huge sales for them. Later, in late October, the cookware would be released in the New York and Philadelphia markets. Test areas of the west coast would get the cookware by the end of the year. Full national distribution would begin in 1959.

A huge promotion campaign was launched to advertise this extra special cookware to consumers. It was emphasized that this cookware was made from Pyroceram®, a special ceramic-glass that was developed to be used to make the nosecones of missiles. The attraction of taking the dishes directly from the freezer to the oven and then the table was a big hit among consumers. The pieces could also be used on the range, since they resisted crazing, cracking, and even scratching. Since the dishes were non-porous, they wouldn't absorb any flavors from what you used in cooking your favorite dish. Another advantage was that they were easy to clean. Special easy lock-on handles could also easily be used for moving the pieces during the cooking process. Sales staff was specifically trained to demonstrate taking the cookware directly from the freezer to range or oven. Showing off the ease of cooking was another plus.

While the promotions were being put in place to launch the Corning Ware®, employees were given a chance to buy this cookware ahead of the public. Stocks of the pieces were offered for sale in employee sales rooms at all the locations. There were only four pieces initially offered. Employees could purchase any of the pieces for half of the retail price. The largest piece was a 10" square, all-purpose dish that had a matching lid and an optional cradle or metal tray serving. Retail price was $10.95 or $12.95 with a cradle. The employee special prices were $5.47 or $6.47, respectively. The next piece was a 1 quart saucepan with a clear Pyrex® lid and a handle at a retail price of $5.95. The third piece was 1-1/2 quart saucepan, also with a clear Pyrex® lid and a handle. This piece retailed for $6.50. The last piece was a

Corning brochure: The most amazing Freeze, Cook, Serve ware that you have ever used. *Reprinted with permission from Corning Incorporated.*

1-3/4 quart saucepan that also had a clear Pyrex® lid and handle. The retail price on this one was $6.95. A special trio combination was offered for the three saucepans, three lids, one cradle and one handle at a retail price of $14.95. In addition, Corning also offered Corning employees the opportunity to buy the cookware as Christmas gifts for family and friends and Corning would mail them out for them. Each of the pieces was packed in a special blue and white decorative box.

A disastrous fire at a Chicago house wares show in 1967 demonstrated the durability of the cookware in a sad way. The whole building and contents was destroyed and yet when the firemen went through the rubble, the cookware survived and showed its real capability. Even though Corning could have used this unfortunate event to capitalize on its special cookware, they decided not to use this information in any of their advertising. The local news, of course, picked up on this story.

Through the years, many different patterns were developed in the cookware. The Blue Cornflower was by far the most popular and lasted the longest. Next was Spice O' Life, followed by Wildflower and Country Festival. This book is organized chronologically based on when the patterns were introduced.

Please enjoy this new valuable reference book as we all celebrate the 50th anniversary of this cookware. At this point we do not consider the cookware to be collectible, as such, but a constant utilitarian item still being used in the kitchen, as it should be. People are adding sizes they never obtained or more pieces of a favorite size. It is sad that this unique cookware is not longer being made, but there are many resources for locating vintage pieces to add to your assortment of cookware. We found that pieces are starting to appear at shows, shops, and malls. There usually are several pieces on eBay in any given week. In addition, some pieces will be able to be found at Replacements, Ltd. if there are enough requests.

Measurements

To ensure that everyone gets a true feel of the size of the pieces, we have measured all the pieces for height, width, and liquid measure, where we could. The height is only of the pan and does not include the lid being on the piece. The width does not include the handles and is taken on the opposite side.

Value Guide

With this being such a new field, it was hard to obtain true accurate values for this cookware. Since it is not really being collected, but rather still being used in the kitchen, prices shown reflect more of a replacement value. Many sources were checked to obtain an average value. We checked at shows, shops and malls along with online shops, eBay and Replacements to determine the values shown.

Marks

Most every piece of Corning is marked. Sometimes it is hard to see, but it is definitely marked. The early pieces were marked on the bottom. Some of the pieces had an embossed style of marking. Cornflower pieces had a blue mark that matched the color of the Cornflower. Other pieces had a gray or black marks on them. At times these are very faint and hard to see. Sometimes you have to hold the piece at an angle to see it. When the style of handle was changed, the markings were on the underside of it. When the liquid measure was switched from pints and quarts to liters, the markings were once again embossed. The mark could be under the handle, on top of the handle or on the bottom of the piece.

The mark generally includes Corning Ware®, a stock number, size, how it could be used and Corning, NY, USA.

We did find one exception to the piece being marked. When a skillet was packaged and sold with the Electromatic skillet, we found the cookware was not marked. All of these skillets have very flat bottoms so they will sit properly on the cook surface. Since the Electromatic was marked with Corning, it was probably felt there was no need to mark the cookware.

Pyroceram™ mark.

History

Amory Houghton, Sr., obtained his first glass making experience by purchasing a stake in a small glass company called Bay State. After this company was sold, Houghton and several other investors founded the Union Glass Company in Somerville, Massachusetts, in 1854. Ten years later, in 1864, Houghton sold his interest in Union Glass, bought Brooklyn Flint Glass, and moved his family to Brooklyn. After facing the high costs of materials and fuel, a decision was made in 1867 to relocate the company to Corning, New York. At that time the company was renamed Corning Flint Glass Works to honor the town it was now part of. After becoming incorporated in 1875, the company was again renamed. This time the company would just be called Corning Glass Works.

The company turned its attention to making specialty glass products that were both pressed and blown. Some of these first products were tableware, cane glass, thermometer and barometer tubing, vial and gauge tubing, druggists' and chemical glassware, and blanks for cut glassware. Light bulbs were also made for Thomas Edison beginning in 1879. After the turn of the century, a railroad light lens was developed that withstood the extreme heat of a flame and yet didn't shatter when rain or snow hit the lens.

A very important technical development was the creation of Pyrex® glass in 1912, which was first marketed in 1915. This was a heat-resistant glass made out of Borosilicate that was designed for baking dishes in the kitchen. An industrial use of Pyrex® came in 1936 when Corning successfully manufactured a 200 inch optical disc for use on the Hale telescope at Mount Palomar in California.

Along the way, Corning has acquired a couple of glass companies. Steuben Glass was purchased in 1918 along with Macbeth-Evans Glass in 1936. The Owens-Corning Fiberglass Corporation was started in 1938.

In the 1940s, Corning was working on more glass items for use in consumer products. A continuous process was developed for making optical glass in 1942. One

Corning Glass Works factory located behind the bridge.

Corning Glass Works factory with rail cars.

of the next creations was the television tube in 1947 that was followed by centrifugal casting in 1949 and color tubes in 1953.

Corning Glass celebrated its Centennial in 1951. To further public knowledge about glass, Corning Glass Works opened their Corning Museum of Glass to commemorate this special milestone in Corning's history.

Donald Stookey at work in the lab. *Photo courtesy of Corning Incorporated, Archives.*

Donald Stookey earned his doctorate in Physical Chemistry from the Massachusetts Institute of Technology in 1940 and went to work for Corning Glass Works that summer. He began his work on researching opal glass. He looked forward to developing new products. One of his first products began with the discovery of FotoForm in 1948. This was glass that was able to be chemically etched. While working with this glass, a temperature gauge malfunctioned and allowed the glass to accidentally reach 900 degrees Celsius. This was the first glass-ceramic product and it was called Fotoceram. Stookey was excited to discover that glass could take on ceramic properties.

Collaboration with the United States military began in World War II, and continued after the war. The military needed a product for use on the Radomes (nosecones) of antiaircraft missiles that was resistant to heat, cold, and corrosion. Stookey continued his work by researching a substance that met these requirements. The new glass-ceramic product that Stookey developed, was given the name of Pyroceram® and the patent, #2,920,971 was given to Corning Glass Works and Donald Stookey in 1956. Pyroceram® is a crystalline ceramic that is made from glass, which is non-crystalline, using the catalyst of titanium oxide. The resulting substance has a low coefficient of expansion which means that it is very resistant to extreme changes in temperatures.

Corning Glass Works factory in Martinsburg, West Virginia.

With Pyroceram® now being part of the space age, attention was turned to using this product in the kitchen. A whole line of cookware was developed that could be taken from the freezer and go straight to the oven. In addition, it was attractive enough to be used as a serving dish to use on the table. The name of Corning Ware® was given to the cookware in 1957. The public was introduced to this new cookware in 1958 and instantly was a huge success. The vacant Paden City Pottery building in Paden City, West Virginia, was first used to mass produce this new cookware. A new plant was built in Martinsburg, West Virginia, and production was transferred there in 1960. The former facility was then used for warehousing the product. In 1962, the Paden City facility was reactivated once again to make Corning Ware®.

Corning Ware® Made in Canada mark.

We also discovered that at some point a plant was operated to make the cookware in Canada. A factory was opened in Leaside, Ontario, which is just outside of Toronto. Leaside was a busy manufacturing town and had the proud distinction of being the site of Canada's first heat resistant glass ware.

As the company was sampling ideas for designs, a shaft of wheat was first suggested. Other companies of the time had a wheat design and several pieces of wheat were made. Unfortunately, Wheat wasn't well received by the public and another design needed to be developed. The first major pattern by Corning was the simple Blue Cornflower that was placed on the white material. The timeless beauty of blue and white had always been popular and so the decision was made to go with the Blue Cornflower. A few pieces of Starburst and Trefoil were also made in those early years.

As time went on other cookware patterns were introduced. The Centura® dinnerware line was first introduced in 1962. Eight years later in 1970, Corelle® dinnerware was put on the market.

While, Corning expanded their consumer line, work also continued in many other directions. Fiber optics were developed in the 1970s along with the ceramic bases of catalytic converters for automobiles. Polychromatic glass was developed in 1978. The 1980s saw the manufacture of LCD glass for flat panel televisions. In 1986, Donald Stookey was honored with the National Medal of Technology. In 1987, dentists could obtain replacement teeth that were developed at Corning. These simulated natural teeth and came with a natural translucent color. In 1989, Corning's name was changed to Corning Incorporated.

The 1990s saw more important technological advances at Corning. NASA launched its Hubble telescope in April 1990. Corning produced the primary mirror blank for it which was made of ultra low expansion glass. This allows the least amount of exposure to temperature changes. To reduce the weight of the glass, honeycomb sections are put in between two light weight glass sheets. The mirror weighs only 1800 pounds instead of 8000 pounds if it were solid glass. In 1994, a mirror blank was made for the Subaru telescope on Mount Mauna Kea in Hawaii. This is the largest piece of glass in the world weighing 35 tons; it is 27 feet wide. That same year, Corning was honored with the National Medal of Technology. In 1995 they were given the Malcolm Baldridge National Quality Award.

Industrial technology was soon becoming a major portion of Corning and the decision was made in 1998 to sell their consumer division to World Kitchen. The rights to the name of Corning Ware®, Corelle®, Visions® and Pyrex® all went to World Kitchen.

Today Corning is a major influence in global industrial research and technology. Their top rated laboratories continue to expand on different uses of specialty glass and ceramics. A recent development was the aluminum titanate filter for the diesel engine. Already they are supplying Cummins, Hyundai, and Kia Motors. As Corning continues to look to the future, a research facility, a few miles from Corning, located in Painted Post, New York, has hundreds of scientists conducting research on numerous ideas.

Corning is still located in Corning, New York. Worldwide, they have about 25,000 employees. Besides research centers in the United States, they are also in both Europe and Asia. Corning, which went public in 1945, trades on the New York Stock Exchange under the symbol of GLW. They are a Fortune 500 company and currently have a rating of 439.Their revenue for 2007 topped over $5.8 billion.

We applaud them for their past developments and look forward to what they will provide for all of us for a better future.

Brochure cover, "Important Tips on use and care of your new Corning Ware® cookware Corning." *Reprinted with permission from Corning Incorporated.*

How Pyroceram® Cookware Is Made

The process of making the Pyroceram® cookware involves many complex steps. The moulds are made and tooled in the Corning mould shop. After the mould is made and approved, it is ready to enter the production stages. Silica sand along with other regular glass ingredients are combined with a nucleating agent. These raw materials being mixed together are called a batch. Next, this batch is put into a melting unit where it will become molten glass-ceramic at around 2300 degrees Fahrenheit.

The special glass-ceramic molten batch is moved into the hub machine. Jim Giffen invented this machine that was first installed at the Martinsburg plant in 1961 and used there for the next 40 years. This machine operates like a Ferris wheel turning with a series of moulds at the end. As the hub turns, a small amount of glass pours in and is shaped inside the mould. Excess glass is cut off allowing the hub to keep rotating. The pieces then enter an annealing lehr. After the pieces emerge from the annealing lehr, they are a crystal glass. An inspector will check the dimension of the piece with a metal gauge. Once the piece passes this stage, it is ready to be decorated.

In the case of the Blue Cornflower, a silk screen design is applied by machine. Many of the decorations use a silk screening process, while others have a decal applied to them. An inspector checks the decoration and it is then placed on a multi-shelf kiln cart. A special vacuum is used to keep these carts clean since any type of debris can interfere with the firing process.

Once the cart is full, a kiln operator pushes the uncerammed pieces into the ceramming kiln. The heat treatment inside this kiln involves a special technique that transforms the actual molecular structure of the piece. After a firing process, the pieces will emerge white and now looks ceramic. The pieces are removed from the cart and placed on a conveyor belt where they travel to another area for a final inspection. After the last quality control, the piece is then packed for shipment.

Patterns

The patterns are arranged chronologically by the year they were first introduced. Some of the patterns ran for many years while others were only offered for a very short time. A detailed photo is given to show each decoration. Dates of production are listed for each pattern. A description of the marks on each piece is provided. There are as many different shapes as we could find for each pattern.

Wheat

Detail of Wheat pattern.

One of the most surprising things we learned while doing research for this book, was that the Blue Cornflower was not the first choice for a decoration on Corning's new cookware. Once the cookware was designed, then a decoration for it needed to be chosen. A simple shaft of wheat was created for the cookware. The wheat design was test marketed in several areas in 1958. Lenox and Hocking's Fire King line each had their own wheat pattern. It was probably felt that Wheat would be a good choice for this new cookware. Unfortunately, the public was not attracted to it and a decision was made to find a new decoration. After the Blue Cornflower was introduced, the Wheat line was dropped.

After the Wheat pattern was discontinued on the Corning Ware®; a Royal Wheat pattern was offered in Pyrex® as part of a promotion in 1961.

Wheat, detail of mark on bottom: Corning Ware® W-41 Petite Pan Made in USA.

Wheat, petite pan, #W-41, 2.25" tall, 5.5" wide, 1 pint, plastic lid, marked on bottom: Corning Ware® W-41 Petite Pan Made in USA, **$6.50**.

Wheat, saucepan, covered, #W-4, 3.25" tall, 6" wide, 7.5" long, 1.5 quart, rectangle, glass lid, marked on the bottom: Corning Ware® W-4 1 ½ qt. Made in USA, **$11.50.**

Wheat, saucepan, covered, #W-1 ¾-B, 2" tall, 7" wide, 1 ¾ quart, glass lid, marked on the bottom: Corning Ware® 1 ¾ QT W-1 ¾-B Made in USA, **$9.50.**

Wheat, detail of mark on bottom: Corning Ware® 1 ¾ QT. W-1 ¾-B Made in USA.

Wheat, skillet, covered, #W-10-B, 2" tall, 10" wide, glass lid, metal cradle 9.5" wide and 13" long, marked on the bottom: Corning Ware® 10 IN W-10-B Made in USA, **$14.50.**

Wheat, teapot, #P-104, 5.25″ tall, 5.5″ wide, 6 cup, marked on the side: Corning Ware® 6 cup, **$9.50.**

Wheat, percolator coffee pot, 10″ tall, 5.5″ wide, 10 cup, marked on the side: Corning Ware® 10 cup, **$12.50**.

Mark on Wheat percolator: Corning Ware® 10 cup.

Blue Cornflower

Detail of Blue Cornflower pattern.

A basic blue and white decoration has always been very popular with the public. After Wheat failed to attract customers, a simple small blue flower decoration was tried against the striking white cookware. The idea for the cornflower came from an item that was found at the local dime store. The pattern was called Blue Cornflower and was introduced in 1958. The public loved it and sales really took off.

The only piece to have a matching lid was the 10" skillet-all purpose dish with a small round knob. All the other items had a crystal lid with a wedge shaped knob. By 1961 the lids were changed to all have a small round knob.

In the first years, there were three covered skillets and four saucepans. A detachable handle could also be purchased to go with each of these. The large 10" skillet and 2.5 quart saucepan could also come with a cradle (metal serving tray). The pieces could be purchased individually or as part of two sets. The Royal Family came with three saucepans (1, 1.5 & 1.75 quarts), 3 lids, one handle, one cradle, plus a deluxe 10" skillet with a matching lid, handle, lid and cradle. The Saucepan set consisted of three dishes (1, 1.5 & 1.75 quarts), three lids, one handle and one cradle.

In 1960 a percolator and teapot were added to the Blue Cornflower line. The next year, in 1961, several more pieces were added. There were a platter, roaster, double boiler, party buffet and an electromatic skillet. A party buffet consisted of a 1.75 quart saucepan with a chrome cradle and candle warmer. Two new sets were also available.

The Chef set included a 1 quart saucepan, 1.5 quart saucepan, 1.75 quart saucepan, 2 quart saucepan, a 10" skillet, 9 cup percolator, two cradles, five Pyrex® lids and a detachable handle. The Homemaker set was available with a 1 quart saucepan, 1.5 quart saucepan, 1.75 quart saucepan, 9" skillet, 6 cup percolator, four Pyrex® lids, a chrome cradle and a detachable handle.

An August, 1962, newspaper announced the premier of a new Pyroceram® dinnerware line. There would be two decorations, the Blue Cornflower, to match the cookware and Pewter Classic. A nationwide unveiling would be during a two hour CBS television program that was sponsored by Corning on September 23, 1962. This show would honor the opening night of the Lincoln Center for the Arts in New York City. Could you imagine how many people watched that program and saw the new Corning dinnerware? What a great exposure for a new product.

Brochure of Blue Cornflower cookware: Corning Ware® Freeze/ Cook/ Serve Ware. *Reprinted with permission from Corning Incorporated.*

Through the years many more pieces were added, until, in 1972, there was a total of 36 different items. These consisted of six covered saucepans, two covered skillets, table saver, handles, sauce maker, Dutch oven, platter, two roasters, three percolators, three teapots, two buffets, five baking dishes, two petite pans, and three menu-ette covered saucepans. Also during 1972, Corning announced a change in their cookware line based on consumer comments and ideas from their test kitchen. The new developments were: flatter bottoms, thinner walls, larger tab handles, and larger knobs on the lids.

The *Gaffer News*, announced a new line called RangeToppers in 1979. The new items would be available in stores starting in early 1980.These pieces look like the regular cookware but would have a thin layer of aluminum that is bonded to the bottom of the Pyroceram®. The pieces were specially designed for use on the range. There were four covered saucepans and two skillets. Scientists at Corning had spent about nine years working on this project to devise a method for bonding the aluminum and Pyroceram® together. Corning was looking to capture part of the cookware market held by Farberware®, Revere Ware® and Club Aluminum®.

By 1988, there were only seven pieces left of Cornflower cookware. By the end of the year the pattern was discontinued. The era of the simple blue and white cornflower was over to make way for the new patterns of soft pastel decorations.

Bakeware

Blue Cornflower, loaf pan, #P-315B, 10.75" long, 5.5" wide, 3.25" tall, 2 quart, plastic lid, marked on bottom: "Corning Ware® P-315B, 9x5x3 inch Range-Oven-Microwave Corning NY USA 178 MA, **$12.50 w/lid; $9.50 w/o lid. Note:** The original plastic cover is hard to find. The loaf pan # is P-315 and when it came with a plastic lid, the number is P-315B.

Blue Cornflower, detail of mark on bottom for loaf pan: Corning Ware® P-315 9x5x3 2 QT Made in USA.

Blue Cornflower, pie plate, #P-309, 10″ wide, 1.5″ tall, **$9.50**. **Left:** Dark blue pattern; **Right:** Regular blue pattern.

Blue Cornflower, pie plate, showing detail of mark on bottom of left one: Corning Ware® P-309 9 in Made in USA For Range & Microwave.

Blue Cornflower. **Top:** baker, #P-322, 2.5″ tall, 8.75″ wide, 9.75″ long, marked on the bottom: P-322 8x8x2 Corning Ware® for range and microwave USA, **$12.50; bottom:** open roaster, #A-76, 2.5″ tall, 12.75″ wide, 16″ long, marked on the bottom: A-76 14 x 11 ½ x 2 ¼ Corning Ware® for range and microwave USA, **$18.50**.

Blue Cornflower, cake dish, #P-321, 2″ tall, 8.75″ wide, round, tab handles, marked on bottom: Corning Ware® P-321 8 IN. Made in USA, **$14.50. Note:** round items are all hard to find.

Detail of mark on bottom: Corning Ware® P-332 12x7 1/2x2 2 QT. Made in USA.

Blue Cornflower, roaster, #P-332, 2.25" tall, 8.5" wide, 13.5" long, marked on bottom: Corning Ware® P-332 12x7 1/2x2 2 QT. Made in USA, **$12.50**.

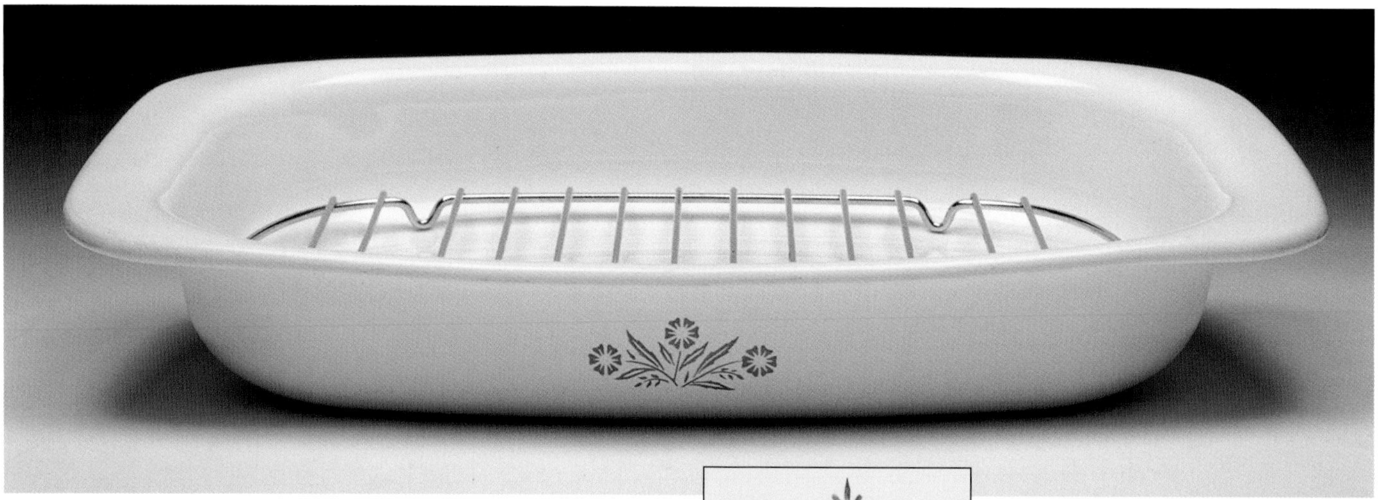

Blue Cornflower, roaster, #P-21, open, 2.25" tall, 10" wide, 15.25" long, oval footed metal rack, 11.75" long, 7.5" wide, marked on bottom: P-21 13x5x2 Corning Ware® For Range and Microwave USA, **$14.50**.

Blue Cornflower, detail of mark on bottom of open roaster: Corning Ware® P-21 Roaster Made in USA.

Blue Cornflower, roaster, #P-76-B, 2.5" tall, 11" wide, 17.25" long, wire rack, marked on the bottom: Corning Ware® P-76-B Roaster Made in USA For Range & Microwave, **$18.50**.

Blue Cornflower, detail of mark on bottom of open roaster: Corning Ware® P-76-B Roaster Made in USA For Range & Microwave.

Blue Cornflower brochure showing beverage makers. *Reprinted with permission from Corning Incorporated.*

Blue Cornflower, teapot, **left**: Original metal infuser, marked on each of the tiers on the lid – 2 cup, 4 cup, 6 cup. Each of the measurements was for how much tea to put in the infuser for the desired amount of tea to brew; **right**: Cornflower, teapot, #P-105, 7.25" tall, 6.5" wide, 2 quart, marked on the side: Corning Ware® 2 qt., **$24.50.**

Blue Cornflower, detail of mark on side of teapot: Corning Ware® 3 cup P-103.

Blue Cornflower, teapots, **left**: #P-103, 4" tall, 4.5" wide, 3 cup, marked on side: Corning Ware® 3 cup P-103, **$12.50**; **right**: #P-104, 5.5" tall, 5.5" wide, 6 cup, marked on side: Corning Ware® 6 cup, **$9.50.**

Blue Cornflower, detail of mark on side of teapot: Corning Ware® 6 cup.

Blue Cornflower, percolator, #P-114-U, 10" tall, 4 cup, glass insert, **$24.50.** Shown apart to show the details of each piece.

CORNING WARE IS WORTH ALL THE LOVING CARE YOU GIVE IT

Cooking Temperature—Corning Ware can take hottest range-top heat, but you should reduce customary cooking temperatures. Heating Corning Ware slowly prevents scorching of food.

Washing—Corning Ware washes spotless in a jiffy. If stubborn stains won't come off with soap and water, rub with sponge and scouring powder. If stains persist, use any good household bleach according to package directions. Do not use metal scouring pads because they leave gray marks on the harder Pyroceram. These marks, however, can be washed off with scouring powder.

Handle—The detachable handle fits every saucepan and skillet and locks securely with a single twist. Always remove handle before placing Corning Ware in oven or under broiler or in the dishwasher.

Candle warmers—Do not drop matches or other foreign material in the candle warmer. Table covering should be kept smooth in the area under the candle warmer.

GUARANTEE

Corning Glass Works, Corning, New York, unconditionally guarantees that any Corning Ware dealer is authorized to replace any Corning Ware that ever breaks from temperature extremes.

Corning Glass Works, Corning, New York — Corning Glass Works of Canada Ltd., Leaside, Ontario

BEST COFFEE YOU EVER DRANK

One secret of good coffee is freshness. The Corning Ware Percolator, being made of Pyroceram, is non-porous . . . can't absorb odors or flavors . . . washes sparkling clean. No leftover, stale taste.

To make refreshing, delicious coffee:

(1) Measure water into percolator according to number of cups of coffee desired. The Corning Ware Percolator has cup markings on the inside for easy measuring. For best results, use full capacity (6 cups in 6-cup percolator, etc.). For smaller amounts, you will need to use proportionately more coffee and allow longer perking time.

The water level should not touch the bottom of the coffee basket. If you use a standard cup measure, put in 6 oz. water for each cup of brew. A cup of coffee as poured is considered to be 5½ oz.

(2) To prevent sediment in coffee, run cold water through the coffee basket before putting in coffee. Then use 2 level tablespoons (1 coffee measure) of regular or percolator grind for each cup of brew desired.

(3) Insert basket assembly into percolator. Cover. Percolate slowly 4 to 7 minutes after water begins perking up into glass knob.

Corning Ware percolators available in 6 and 9 cup sizes.

PERFECT CUP OF TEA EVERY TIME

Bring freshly drawn cold water to a brisk boil right in the Corning Ware Teapot. Take off the range and add tea—loose, in tea bags, or in metal tea ball. Use 1 rounded teaspoonful tea to every 6 oz. of water. Steep 3 to 5 minutes. Remove tea leaves. Then pour the finest cup of tea ever.

Teapot capacity: 6 cups

Blue Cornflower brochure showing a teapot and percolator. *Reprinted with permission from Corning Incorporated.*

Blue Cornflower, percolators. **Left:** #P-149, 9 cup, 10″ tall, 5.5″ wide at base, marked on side: Corning Ware® 9 cup, **$12.50; center:** #P-116, 6 cup, 8.25″ tall, 4.75″ wide at base, marked on side: Corning Ware® 6 cup, **$12.50; right:** #P-80-EP, 10.25″ tall, 5″ wide at base, electric, marked on side: Corning Ware® 10 cup P-80-EP, **$14.50.**

Blue Cornflower, percolator, #P-116, 6 cup, 8.25″ tall, 4.75″ wide at base, marked on side: Corning Ware® 6 cup, **$12.50.** **Note:** Shown apart with all of its pieces.

Blue Cornflower, percolator, #P-149, 9 cup, 10″ tall, 5.5″ wide at base, marked on side: Corning Ware® 9 cup, **$12.50.** **Note:** Shown apart with all of its pieces.

Blue Cornflower, percolator, #P-80-EP, 10 cup, 10.25" tall, 5" wide at base, electric, marked on side: Corning Ware® 10 cup P-80-EP, **$16.50.** **Note:** Shown apart with all of its pieces including the hard to find trivet.

Blue Cornflower, beverage server, #P-504, 7.25" tall, 5" wide, 8 cup, marked on side: Corning Ware® 8 cup, **$19.50**.

Blue Cornflower, mug, 3.75" tall, 3.15" wide, **$7.50.**

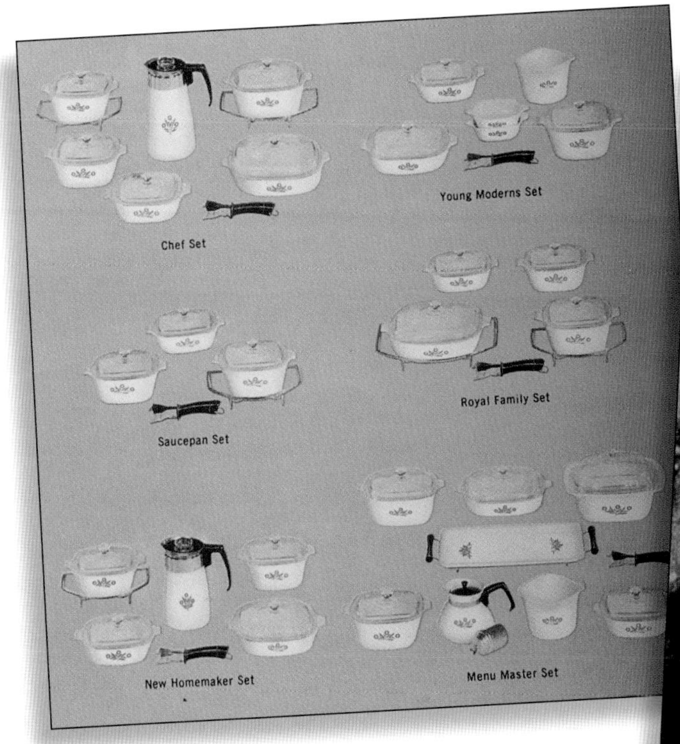

Blue Cornflower brochure showing sets you could buy: Chef's set; Saucepan set; Homemaker set; Young Modern's set; Royal Family set; Menu Master set. *Reprinted with permission from Corning Incorporated.*

Blue Cornflower brochure showing ice to flame photo. *Reprinted with permission from Corning Incorporated.*

Blue Cornflower.
Left: lobster chef holding vegetables; **right:** saucepan with lid, #P-4-B, 1 ½ quart.

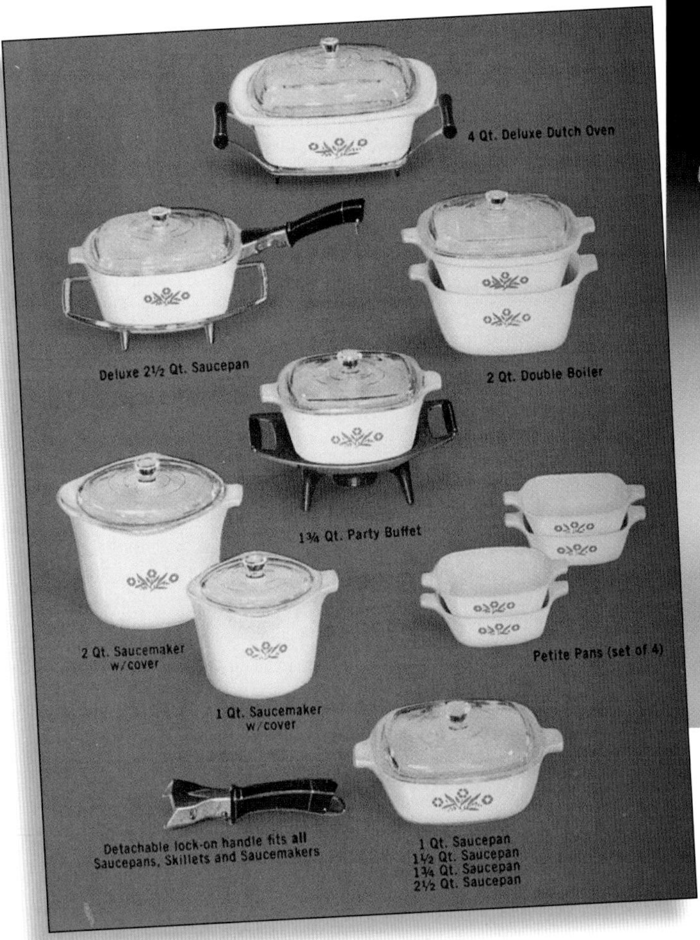

Blue Cornflower brochure showing assortment of saucepans. *Reprinted with permission from Corning Incorporated*.

Blue Cornflower, petite pans. **Top**: #P-43-B, 2.25" tall, 5.25" wide, 22 ounce, marked on the bottom: Corning Ware® P-43-B 22 oz. Made in USA, glass lid, **$9.50; bottom**: #P-43-B, 2.25" tall, 5.25" wide, 22 ounce, marked on the bottom: Corning Ware® P-43-B 22 oz. made in USA, plastic lid, **$7.50.**

Blue Cornflower, petite pan, showing bottom mark: Corning Ware® P-41-B 12 oz. made in USA for Range & Micro-wave.

Blue Cornflower, petite pans. **Left**: #P-43-B, 2.25" tall, 5.25" wide, 22 ounce, marked on the bottom: Corning Ware® P-43-B 22 oz. Made in USA, plastic lid, **$7.50; right**: #P-41-B, 1.5" tall, 5.25" wide, 12 ounce, marked on the bottom: Corning Ware® P-41-B 12 oz. made in USA for Range & Microwave, plastic lid, **$6.50.**

Blue Cornflower, saucepan with glass wedge lid, #P-11-1, 2" tall, 7" wide, 1 quart, marked on the bottom: Corning Ware® For range & microwave USA, **$8.50**. **Note:** The wedge lids are harder to find.

Blue Cornflower, detail of mark on bottom: Corning Ware® P-7-B 7 IN. Made in USA For Range & Microwave.

Blue Cornflower. **Left**: skillet, #P-7-B, 1.5" tall, 7" wide, 1.5 pint, glass lid, marked on bottom: Corning Ware® P-7-B 7 IN Made in USA, marked on lid: P-7-C, **$8.50; right**: saucepan with lid, #A-1-B, 1 quart, 2" tall, 7" wide, glass lid, marked on handle: Corning Ware® A-1-B 1 Quart Range – Oven – Microwave Corning NY USA 279MA, **$8.50**.

Inset, top:
Blue Cornflower, detail of mark on underside of handle: Corning Ware® A-1-B 1 Quart Range – Oven – Microwave Corning, NY, USA 11180 MA.

Blue Cornflower, saucepan with lid, #A-1 ½-B, 2.75" tall, 7" wide, 1.5 liter, molded plastic lid, marked on the underside of the handles on one side: Corning Ware®, on the other – A-1 ½-B 1.5 liter, **$8.50. Note:** This has a newer plastic lid.

Blue Cornflower, saucepan with lid, #C-40, 3.25" tall, 7" wide, 1.5 quart, glass lid, embossed on bottom: Corning Pyroceram™ Made in USA C-40, **$8.50.**

Blue Cornflower, saucepan with glass lid, #A-4, 2.75" tall, 7" wide, 1.25 quart, marked on the bottom: Corning Pyroceram™ Made in USA A-4, **$8.50.**

Blue Cornflower, saucepan with lid, #A-1 ½ -B, 3″ tall, 7″ wide, 1.5 quart, glass lid, marked on bottom: Corning Ware® 1 ½ QT. P-1 ½-B Made in USA, **$8.50**.

Blue Cornflower, detail of bottom mark: Corning Ware® 1 ½ QT. P-1 ½-B Made in USA.

Blue Cornflower, saucepans, comparison with handles. **Left**: #P-1 ¾ -B, 3.5″ tall, 7″ wide, 1.75 quarts, **$14.50; right**: #P-43-B, 2.25″ tall, 5.25″ wide, 2.75 cups, **$14.50.**

Blue Cornflower, saucepans with glass lids. **Back:** #P-1 ¾-B, 3.5″ tall, 7.25″ wide, 1 ¾ quart, marked on bottom: Corning Ware® P-1 ¾-B 1 ¾ QT. Made in USA; set in metal cradle, marked on bottom: Corning Ware® P-11-M, **$12.50**. **Left:** #A-1-B, 2″ tall, 7.25″ wide, 1 quart, marked on bottom: Corning Ware® 1 QT., **$7.50. Right**: #P-1 ½ -B, 2.75″ tall, 7″ wide, 1.5 quart, marked on bottom: Corning Ware® P– 1 ½-B 1 ½ QT. Made in USA, **$8.50** .

Blue Cornflower, saucepan with lid, #P-1 ¾-B, 3.5″ tall, 7.25″ wide, 1 ¾ quart, glass lid, marked on bottom: Corning Ware® P-1 ¾-B 1 ¾ QT. Made in USA; set in metal cradle, marked on bottom: Corning Ware® P-11-M-1, **$11.50.**

Blue Cornflower, detail of mark on bottom: Corning Ware® P-1 ¾-B 1 ¾ QT. Made in USA For Range & Microwave.

Blue Cornflower advertising: Corning Cooking in the 1970s special offer.

Blue Cornflower brochure: Corning Welcomes you to cooking in the '70s, front cover. *Reprinted with permission from Corning Incorporated.*

Blue Cornflower, saucepan with glass lid, #P-2 ½-B, 3.5" tall, 8.5" wide, 2 ½ quart, metal cradle, 11.5" long, 8" wide, 2.5" tall, marked on bottom: P 2 ½-B 2 ½ QT. Made in USA For Range & Microwave, **$13.50**.

Blue Cornflower, detail of bottom mark: P 2 ½-B 2 ½ QT. Made in USA For Range & Microwave.

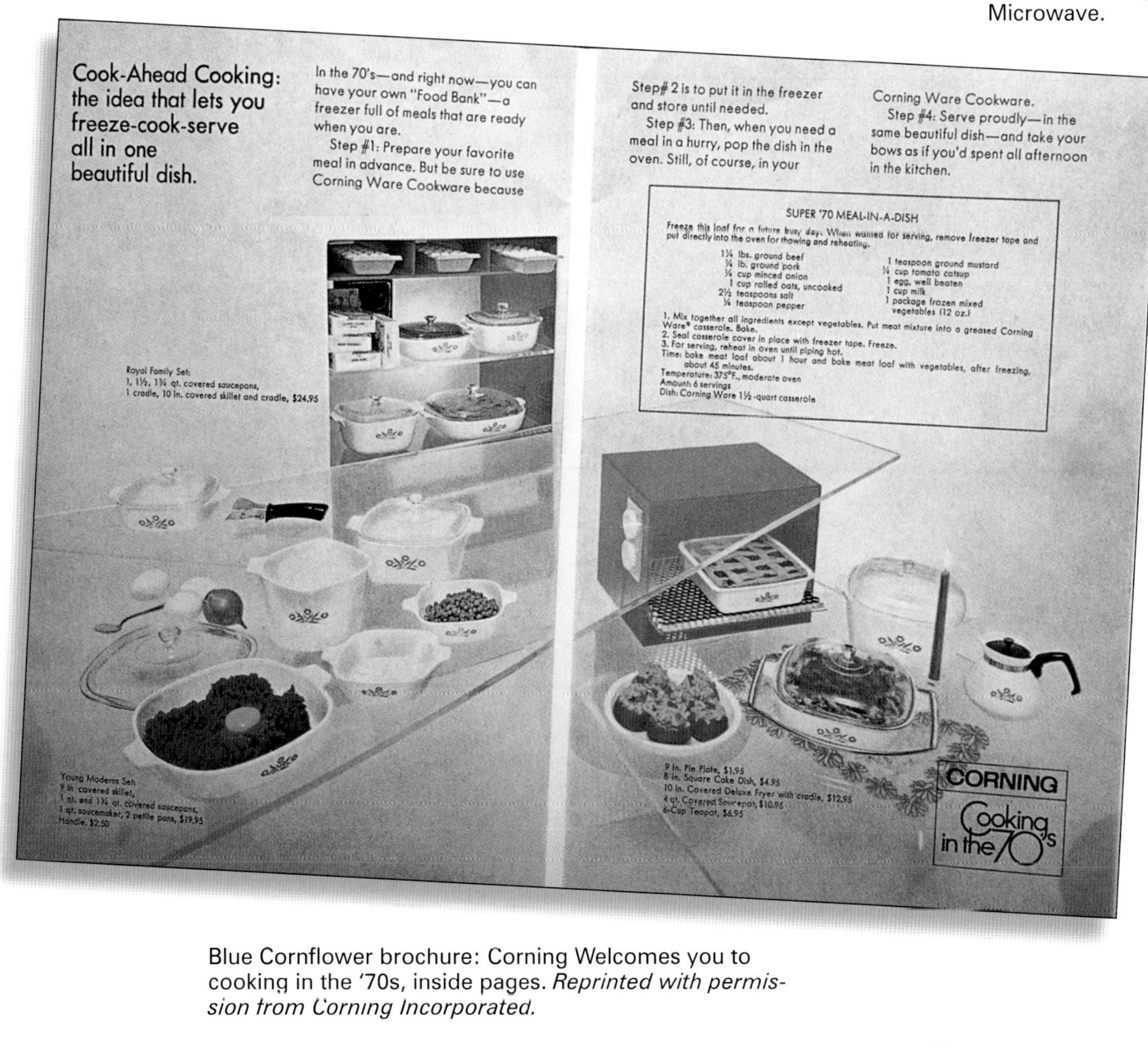

Cook-Ahead Cooking: the idea that lets you freeze-cook-serve all in one beautiful dish.

In the 70's—and right now—you can have your own "Food Bank"—a freezer full of meals that are ready when you are.

Step #1: Prepare your favorite meal in advance. But be sure to use Corning Ware Cookware because

Step# 2 is to put it in the freezer and store until needed.

Step #3: Then, when you need a meal in a hurry, pop the dish in the oven. Still, of course, in your Corning Ware Cookware.

Step #4: Serve proudly—in the same beautiful dish—and take your bows as if you'd spent all afternoon in the kitchen.

SUPER '70 MEAL-IN-A-DISH

Freeze this loaf for a future busy day. When wanted for serving, remove freezer tape and put directly into the oven for thawing and reheating.

- 1¼ lbs. ground beef
- ¼ lb. ground pork
- ¼ cup minced onion
- 1 cup rolled oats, uncooked
- 2½ teaspoons salt
- ¼ teaspoon pepper
- 1 teaspoon ground mustard
- ¼ cup tomato catsup
- 1 egg, well beaten
- 1 cup milk
- 1 package frozen mixed vegetables (12 oz.)

1. Mix together all ingredients except vegetables. Put meat mixture into a greased Corning Ware® casserole. Bake.
2. Seal casserole cover in place with freezer tape. Freeze.
3. For serving, reheat in oven until piping hot.

Time: bake meat loaf about 1 hour and bake meat loaf with vegetables, after freezing, about 45 minutes.
Temperature: 375°F., moderate oven
Amount: 6 servings
Dish: Corning Ware 1½-quart casserole

Royal Family Set:
1, 1½, 1¾ qt. covered saucepans,
1 cradle, 10 in. covered skillet and cradle, $24.95

Young Moderns Set:
9 in. covered skillet,
1 qt. and 1¾ qt. covered saucepans,
1 qt. saucemaker, 2 petite pans, $19.95
Handle, $2.50

9 in. Pie Plate, $1.95
8 in. Square Cake Dish, $4.95
10 in. Covered Deluxe Fryer with cradle, $12.95
4 qt. Covered Saucepot, $10.95
6-Cup Teapot, $6.95

CORNING
Cooking in the 70's

Blue Cornflower brochure: Corning Welcomes you to cooking in the '70s, inside pages. *Reprinted with permission from Corning Incorporated.*

Above:
Blue Cornflower, saucepan with lid, #P-4-B, 3.25" tall, 6.25" wide, 7.75" long, 1.5 quart, glass lid, rectangle shaped, marked on bottom: Corning Ware®, P-4-B 1 ½ QT. Made in USA, **$11.50.**

Below:
Blue Cornflower, saucepans with glass lids. **Back:** #P-2 ½-B, 3.5" tall, 8.5" wide, 2 ½ quart. **$12.50. Front left**: P-1 ¾ -B, 3.5" tall, 7" wide, 1 ¾ quart, **$9.50; front right**: #P-1 ½ -B .75" tall, 7" wide, 1 ½ quart, **$8.50.**

Blue Cornflower, double boiler, **top:** #P-17-B, 4.25" tall, 8.75" wide, 1.75 quart insert; **bottom:** #P-2 ½-B, 2.5 quart bottom, glass lid, **$24.50.**

Blue Cornflower, detail of bottom mark: Corning Ware® P-17-B.

Blue Cornflower, saucepan with lid, #A-3-B, 3.85" tall, 8.5" wide, 3 quart, glass lid, marked under handle: Corning Ware® A-3-B 3 quart Range-Oven-Microwave Corning NY USA 479MA, **$14.50.**

Blue Cornflower, Dutch oven, #P-84-B, 6.75" tall, 12" wide, 4 quart, marked on underside of lip edge: Corning Ware P-84-B 4 QT. Made in USA For range and Microwave, **$19.50. Note:** We also found some with another mark of: Corning Ware Dutch Oven P-34-B 4 qt Made in USA.

Blue Cornflower, detail of mark on bottom: Corning Ware® P-84-B 4 QT. Made in USA For range and Microwave.

Blue Cornflower, saucepans with glass lids. **Top:** #A-5-B, 4.25" tall, 10.25" wide, 5 quart, marked on bottom: Corning Ware® A-5-B 5 Qt. For range & Microwave USA, **$22.50. Bottom:** #P-4-B, 4.25" tall, 10.25" wide, 4 quart, marked on bottom: Corning Ware® P-4-B 4 QT. Made in USA for range and Microwave, **$19.50. Note:** We could find no differences in the sizes of these two and yet they measured different amounts.

Blue Cornflower, saucepans, glass lids, comparison of size. **Left:** #A-5-B, 4.25″ tall, 10.25″ wide, 5 liter, **$22.50; right:** #P-43-B, 2.25″ tall, 5.25″ wide, 2.75 cups, **$14.50.**

Blue Cornflower, saucepan with lid, #A-5-B, 4.25″, 10.75″ wide, 5 quart, marked on bottom: marked on bottom: Corning Ware® A-5-B 5 Qt. For range & Microwave USA; on metal white cooking tray, P-12-ES-N, marked on side bottom: Corning Ware® electric skillet Model P-12-FS-N 120V1400W AC only Do Not Immerse in Water Caution: Use with Wall Base or range receptacle only, **$29.50.**

Blue Cornflower, sauce maker, #P-65, 5.25" tall, 8.75" wide, 2 quart, 3 spouts, marked on the side: Corning Ware® 2 QT. sauce maker, **$19.50.**

Blue Cornflower, sauce maker with glass lid, #P-64-B, 1 quart, 6" tall, 6.75" wide to tab handle, 3 spouts, clip on black handle, marked on side with Corning Ware® P-64-B 1 qt. Made in USA for range & microwave, **$19.50. Note:** We have also found other pieces to have side marks of: Corning Ware® P-55-B 1 qt. Saucemaker. The lid to the three spouted sauce maker is extremely hard to find.

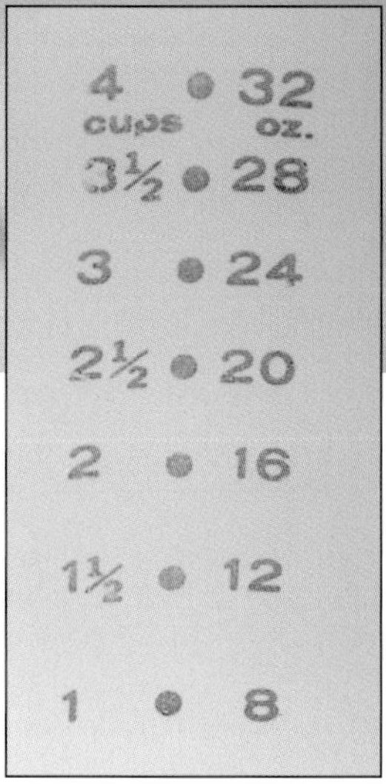

Blue Cornflower, sauce maker, detail of interior mark: on left side: 1 cup to 4 cup; and on right side: 8 oz to 32 oz.

Blue Cornflower, sauce maker, detail of exterior side mark: Corning Ware® P-64-B 1 qt. Made in USA For Range & Microwave.

Blue Cornflower, saucepans with glass lids. **Left:** #P-81-B, 2.15" tall, 5.85" wide, marked on bottom: P-81-B 1 pint, Corning Ware® For range & microwave USA, **$7.50; right:** #P-82, 2.5" tall, 6" wide 1 ½ pint, marked on bottom: Corning Ware® P-82-B 1 ½ pt Made in USA For range & microwave, **$8.50.**

Blue Cornflower, detail of bottom mark: Corning Ware® P-82-B 1 ½ pt Made in USA For range & microwave.

Blue Cornflower, saucepan, #P-89-B, 2.5 cup, 2.5" tall, 6" wide, spouted, marked on bottom: Corning Ware® P-89-B, **$6.50.**

Blue Cornflower, **left**: #P-82-B, saucepan with glass lid, 2.5" tall, 1.5 pint, marked on bottom: "Corning Ware® P-82-B range-oven-microwave, Corning NY USA 182MA, **$8.50; right**: #P-83-B, skillet with glass lid, 1.5" tall, 6" wide, 1 pint, marked on bottom: Corning Ware® P-83-B 6.5 inch range – oven-microwave Corning NY USA 182 MA, **$8.50.**

16 graham crackers
⅓ cup butter
½ cup sugar
1 pkg. (8 oz.) cream cheese
½ cup sugar
2 eggs
1 can (1 lb., 6 oz.) cherry pie filling*

CHERRY TORTE

Start your oven at 325F or slow. Crush graham crackers with a rolling pin. Melt butter on top of range in your 10 inch Corning Ware Skillet. Remove from heat. Mix in crumbs and ½ cup sugar well. Pat mixture on bottom of skillet firmly. Bring cream cheese to room temperature and beat until smooth with a rotary or electric beater. Beat in ½ cup sugar gradually. Add eggs, one at a time, beating hard after each addition. Beat until mixture is very smooth. Pour over crumbs and bake 25 minutes. Remove from oven and cool (if you're in a hurry take Corning Ware Skillet straight from oven to refrigerator). Spoon cherry pie filling (blueberry pie filling is equally delicious) over top and chill in refrigerator 3 hours or overnight. Good-looking Corning Ware goes right to the table. Serves 8 more than generously.

*Note: This is fruit-pie filling, not canned fruit.

Deluxe 10" Skillet complete with bowl, handle, cover, cradle.

¼ cup butter
3 to 3½ lb. chicken, cut in pieces
2 onions
1 clove garlic
2 strips bacon
½ cup cider
1 bouillon cube
¼ teaspoon salt
Dash pepper
Few sprigs parsley
Bay leaf
3 medium onions
3 medium carrots
2 small turnips
½ cup peas, fresh or frozen

COUNTRY CHICKEN

Melt half the butter in a 10 inch Corning Ware Skillet. Add chicken pieces, several at a time, and fry over moderate heat until golden. Set aside. Place 2 finely chopped onions, chopped garlic, bacon cut into pieces in 2½ qt. Corning Ware Saucepan. Fry until onions are limp. Add cider, bouillon cube dissolved in ½ cup boiling water, salt, pepper, parsley sprigs, bay leaf. Simmer a few minutes. Add chicken to mixture, cover and bake in a preheated, slow oven (325F) for 1 hour or until tender.

About 15 minutes before serving melt remaining butter in a small Corning Ware Saucepan. Add the onions, carrots, turnips, all thinly sliced. Add peas along with ¼ cup of the liquid in which the chicken simmered. Cover and cook over a low heat, stirring occasionally, until vegetables are tender. To serve, spoon vegetables around chicken. Serves 4 to 6. Country Chicken, without the vegetable decor, can be frozen.

Deluxe 2½ qt. Saucepan complete with bowl, handle, cover, cradle.

Blue Cornflower brochure showing casseroles and recipes to use. *Reprinted with permission from Corning Incorporated.*

Skillets

Blue Cornflower, detail of the bottom mark: Corning Ware® P-9-B 8 In Made in USA For Range & Microwave.

Blue Cornflower, detail of the mark underneath the handle: Corning Ware® A-8-B 8x8x1 ¾ Range-Oven-Microwave Corning, NY USA 11180MA.

Blue Cornflower, skillets with glass lids. **Left:** #P-9-B, 2" tall, 8.5" wide, 1.5 quarts, marked on bottom: Corning Ware® P-9-B 8 In Made in USA For Range & Microwave, **$9.50; right:** A-8-B, 2" tall, 8.5" wide, 1.5 quart, marked on the underside of handle: Corning Ware® A-8-B 8x8x 1 ¾ inch Range-Oven-Microwave Corning, NY USA 11180MA, **$9.50. Note:** The one on the left is the earlier version and has a small Cornflower. Notice the inward taper of the left one compared to the more squared sides of the right one.

Blue Cornflower Skillets: **back:** 10" with solid glass lid, 2" tall, 9.75" wide, marked on bottom: Corning Pyroceram™ Made in USA B-3, **$14.50. Note:** Matching solid non-transparent lid is hard to find. **Front left:** 2.25" tall, 7" wide, 1 qt. glass lid, marked on bottom: 1 qt. Corning Ware® Pyroceram™ Made in USA, **$8.50; front right:** 2" tall, 8.5" wide, glass lid, marked on bottom: Corning Ware® P-9-B 9 IN Made in USA For Range & Microwave, **$9.50.**

Blue Cornflower, skillet with glass lid, #P-9-B, 2" tall, 8.75" wide, narrow handles, marked on bottom: Corning Ware® P-9-B 9 IN, Made in USA, **$9.50**.

Blue Cornflower, detail of mark on bottom: Corning Ware® P-9-B 9 IN. Made in USA.

Blue Cornflower, skillet with glass lid, #B-10-B, 2" tall, 10" wide, has narrow handles, marked on bottom: Corning Ware® B-10-B 10 IN. skillet, MADE IN USA, **$12.50**.

Blue Cornflower, detail of mark on bottom: Corning Ware® B-10-B 10 IN. skillet, MADE IN USA.

Blue Cornflower, skillet with glass lid, #A-10-B, 2" tall, 10.25" wide, has wide handles, marked on the underside of the handle: Corning Ware® A-10-B 10x10x2 Range-Oven-Microwave Corning, NY USA 1180MA, **$12.50**.

Blue Cornflower, detail of mark underside of the handle: Corning Ware® A-10-B 10x10x2 in Range-Oven-Microwave Corning, NY USA 1180MA.

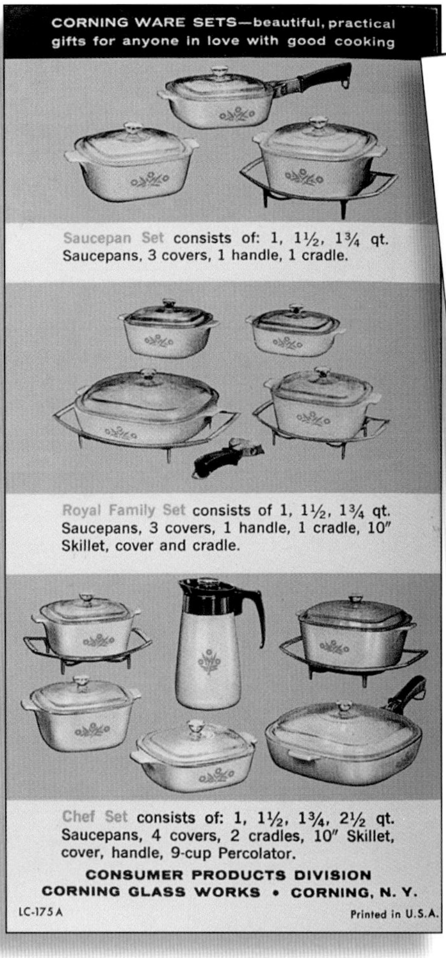

CORNING WARE SETS—beautiful, practical gifts for anyone in love with good cooking

Saucepan Set consists of: 1, 1½, 1¾ qt. Saucepans, 3 covers, 1 handle, 1 cradle.

Royal Family Set consists of 1, 1½, 1¾ qt. Saucepans, 3 covers, 1 handle, 1 cradle, 10" Skillet, cover and cradle.

Chef Set consists of: 1, 1½, 1¾, 2½ qt. Saucepans, 4 covers, 2 cradles, 10" Skillet, cover, handle, 9-cup Percolator.

CONSUMER PRODUCTS DIVISION
CORNING GLASS WORKS • CORNING, N. Y.

LC-175A

Printed in U.S.A.

Blue Cornflower brochure: Corning Ware® sets- beautiful, practical gifts for anyone in love with good cooking. *Reprinted with permission from Corning Incorporated.*

FRENCH DEEP-DISH APPLE PIE

Pastry for a 2 crust pie
Grated rind of ½ lemon
3 large baking apples
½ cup sugar
¼ teaspoon nutmeg
¼ teaspoon cinnamon
Dash salt
1 tablespoon flour
½ cup raisins
¾ cup confectioners' sugar
¼ teaspoon vanilla extract

Make pastry, your own or a mix, and add grated lemon rind to the mixture. Divide in half. Roll one half on a lightly floured board and line a 1 quart Corning Ware Saucepan. Refrigerate remaining pastry and lined saucepan while you make the filling.

Pare, core, and slice apples thinly. Mix sugar, nutmeg, cinnamon, and salt together. Mix flour and raisins together. Put half the apple slices in the pastry lined saucepan. Sprinkle with part of the sugar mixture, and all the raisin mixture. Layer remaining apples and sugar, and cover with top crust, slashed in several places. Bake in a preheated, moderate oven (350F) for 50 to 60 minutes or until pastry is golden. Cool. If you're in a rush, cool in refrigerator immediately.

Last step: Make a smooth mixture of confectioners' sugar, 2 teaspoons water and vanilla. Dribble this frosting over cold pie and serve right from the Corning Ware Saucepan. Serves 4 to 6.

ITALIAN MEAT LOAF

2 slices rye bread
2 slices white bread
1 medium onion
4 sprigs parsley
1 lb. ground beef
3 tablespoons grated Parmesan cheese
1 egg
1 teaspoon salt
¼ teaspoon pepper
2 tablespoons butter
1 can (8 oz.) tomato sauce
1 teaspoon oregano

Put slices of rye and white bread in a 9 inch Corning Ware Skillet. Pour 1 cup water over bread. When soaked, crumble into fine pieces with your hands. Combine with chopped onion, chopped parsley, beef, grated cheese, slightly beaten egg, salt, pepper, and mix thoroughly. Shape mixture into a loaf right in the Corning Ware Skillet. Dot top with butter, and bake, uncovered, in a preheated, moderate oven (350F) for 30 minutes. Pour tomato sauce over loaf, sprinkle with oregano, and continue baking 20 minutes longer. Bring to the table in your attractive Corning Ware Skillet. Serves 4 to 6. Superb either hot or cold.

Note: To freeze, bake meat loaf only 30 minutes. Omit sauce and oregano. Freeze in Corning Ware Skillet. When wanted for serving, pour tomato sauce over frozen meat loaf, sprinkle with oregano, and place in (350F) oven. Bake until hot throughout, about 1 hour.

Skillets available in 7, 9, 10 and 11 inch sizes.

Blue Cornflower brochure showing a casserole and skillet with recipes to use. *Reprinted with permission from Corning Incorporated.*

Blue Cornflower, skillet, #P-910-B, shown upright to show shape and handle.

Blue Cornflower, skillet, #P-910-B, 1.75" tall, 10.25" wide, spouts on each side, gourmet style, black handle, marked on bottom: Corning Ware® P-910-B 10" skillet USA, **$18.50.**

The Mini-Kitchen: the only Electric Skillet that's a complete cook-and-serve system.

You plug it in and it's frying, grilling, braising, boiling or stewing. All automatically...accurately...perfectly.

Lift the 10 inch skillet from the specially designed heater base and your cooking dish becomes a handsome serving dish.

It's the Corning Ware Electromatic Skillet, a "Mini-Kitchen" in gleaming, easy-to-clean Pyroceram® glass ceramic.

The perfect companion piece: A Corning Ware Electromatic Platter.

STEW-FOR-THE-CREW

The aroma of this stew as it cooks in the Corning Ware® Electromatic Skillet will whet even a jaded appetite.

2 tablespoons butter or margarine	1 bay leaf
½ cup chopped onion	4 celery tops
1½ lbs. hamburger	6 sprigs parsley
1 can tomatoes (1 lb., 12 oz.)	2 teaspoons salt
1 can consommé (10½ oz.)	½ teaspoon ground thyme
	¼ teaspoon pepper
	½ teaspoon sugar

3 medium size carrots, sliced

1. Preheat CORNING WARE Electromatic Skillet to 275. Put in butter and chopped onion and cook until onion is golden color, about five minutes.
2. Raise temperature setting to 325. Stir in hamburger and cook until meat is browned, about 10 minutes.
3. Add all remaining ingredients. Cover. Lower temperature setting to 225, and cook one hour longer.

Time: cook about 1 hour and 15 minutes in all
Setting: 275 for browning onion
325 for browning meat
225 for cooking stew
Amount: 6 to 8 servings
Dish: CORNING WARE Electromatic Skillet

16 in. Electromatic Platter, $19.95

10 in. Electromatic Skillet, $29.95

Corning promises to replace any Corning Ware product that ever breaks from temperature extremes upon return of the pieces to a Corning Ware Products Dealer. Furthermore, any imperfect mechanical or electrical part will be replaced free within one year from date of purchase.

The Return of Real Coffee: space-age coffeepots bring back the flavor you've been missing.

You can make real coffee in just a few minutes longer than it takes you to make today's instants and freeze-drieds.

You do it with a Corning Ware® coffeemaker, either regular or electric. That's because with Corning Ware coffeemakers you taste the coffee, not the pot. The reason: coffee oils and odors don't cling to Pyroceram® material, the unique, nonporous material Corning—and only Corning—uses to make coffeemakers.

The Pyroceram material also makes cleaning easy so every Corning Ware coffeemaker washes sparkling clean in minutes . . . even the heaters in our Electromatic models are completely immersible.

CREATING WITH COFFEE

Café au Lait: In true continental style, pour equal amounts of steaming milk and coffee into cups.

Caffè Cappuccino: In Italian-style, combine equal parts of steaming coffee and hot milk. Pour into cups and sprinkle with cinnamon and nutmeg. Serve with sugar.

Mocha Java: Pour equal amounts of hot coffee and hot cocoa into mugs. Top with whipped cream or marshmallows and stir with a cinnamon stick.

4-Cup All White Percolator, $9.95

6-Cup Avocado Medallion Percolator, $10.95

10-Cup Electromatic Percolator, $29.95

CORNING
Cooking

Blue Cornflower brochure: Corning Cooking in the '70s. *Reprinted with permission from Corning Incorporated.*

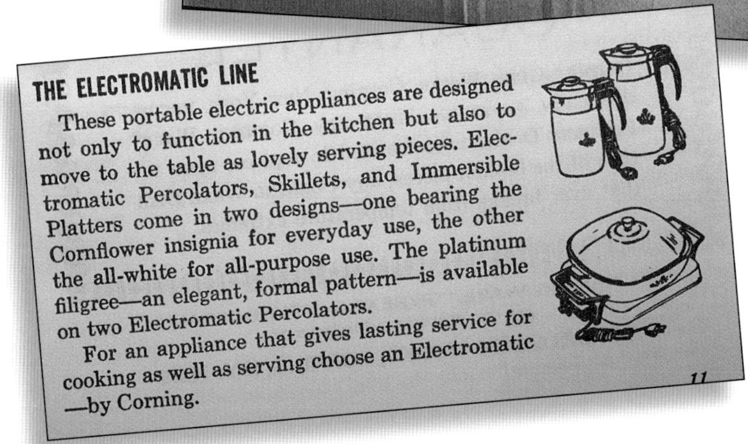

THE ELECTROMATIC LINE

These portable electric appliances are designed not only to function in the kitchen but also to move to the table as lovely serving pieces. Electromatic Percolators, Skillets, and Immersible Platters come in two designs—one bearing the Cornflower insignia for everyday use, the other the all-white for all-purpose use. The platinum filigree—an elegant, formal pattern—is available on two Electromatic Percolators.

For an appliance that gives lasting service for cooking as well as serving choose an Electromatic—by Corning.

11

Corning brochure, "Use & Care of Corning Ware® Cookware" – The Electromatic® Line. *Reprinted with permission from Corning Incorporated.*

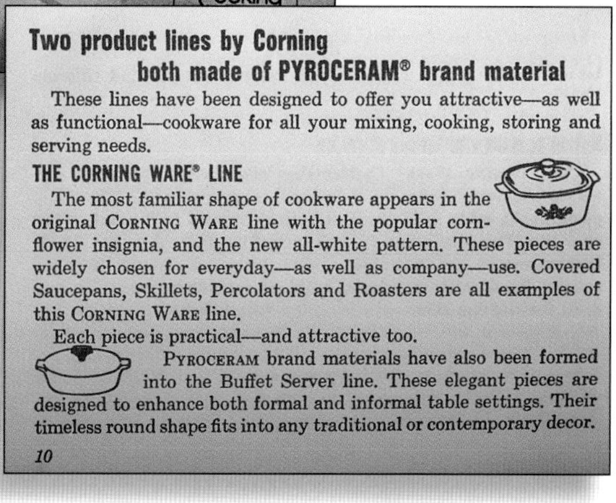

Two product lines by Corning both made of PYROCERAM® brand material

These lines have been designed to offer you attractive—as well as functional—cookware for all your mixing, cooking, storing and serving needs.

THE CORNING WARE® LINE

The most familiar shape of cookware appears in the original CORNING WARE line with the popular cornflower insignia, and the new all-white pattern. These pieces are widely chosen for everyday—as well as company—use. Covered Saucepans, Skillets, Percolators and Roasters are all examples of this CORNING WARE line.

Each piece is practical—and attractive too.

PYROCERAM brand materials have also been formed into the Buffet Server line. These elegant pieces are designed to enhance both formal and informal table settings. Their timeless round shape fits into any traditional or contemporary decor.

10

Corning brochure, "Use & Care of Corning Ware® Cookware" – The Corning Ware® Line." *Reprinted with permission from Corning Incorporated.*

Top: Blue Cornflower, skillet, covered, #A-22-B, 2" tall, 10.25" wide, glass lid, marked on the handle: A-22-B; **bottom**: Electromatic® skillet, white, #P-12-ES-N, 2" tall, 9.75" wide. **$35.00 set.**

Trays

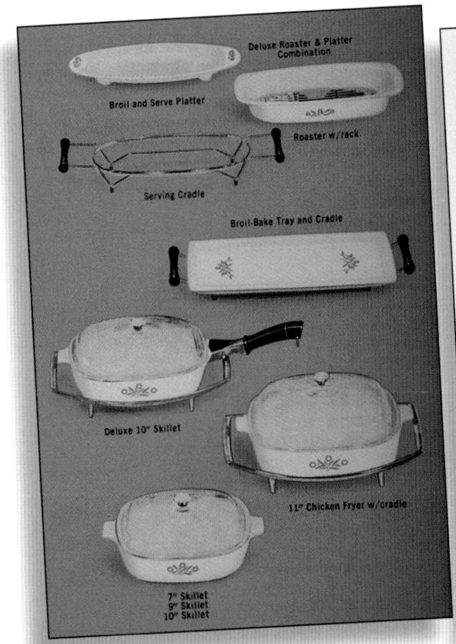

Blue Cornflower, Corning brochure showing platter, roaster, tray and skillets. *Reprinted with permission from Corning Incorporated.*

CORNING WARE® ELECTROMATICS

CORNING WARE Electromatic Percolators in 6 cup and 10 cup sizes.
CORNING WARE Electromatic Skillet.
CORNING WARE Electromatic Immersible Platter.
Foods stay hot right on platter. Keeps dishes at serving temperature.

CORNING WARE® GUARANTEE

Corning Glass Works, Corning, New York, unconditionally guarantees that any CORNING WARE® Dealer is authorized to replace, upon return of all the broken pieces, any CORNING WARE® product that ever breaks from temperature extremes.

ELECTROMATICS GUARANTEE

Corning Glass Works, Corning, New York, unconditionally guarantees that any CORNING WARE® Dealer is authorized to replace any CORNING WARE® product that ever breaks from temperature extremes upon return of all the broken pieces. Furthermore, any CORNING WARE® Dealer is authorized to replace any mechanical or electrical part within one year from date of purchase if not mechanically or electrically perfect.

CONSUMER PRODUCTS DIVISION • CORNING GLASS WORKS • CORNING, NEW YORK

LC-175-E

Printed in U.S.A.

Blue Cornflower, Corning brochure showing Electromatic®. *Reprinted with permission from Corning Incorporated.*

Blue Cornflower, meat platter, #P-19, 16.5" long, 10.25" wide, marked on bottom: "Corning Ware® P-19 platter Made in USA; cradle, P-21-M, 19.5" long, 9.25" wide, **$16.00.**

Blue Cornflower, detail of mark on bottom of platter: Corning Ware® P-19 Platter Made in USA.

Blue Cornflower, tray, #P-35-B, 16" long, 10.5" wide, 1" tall, Broil Bake, **$16.00.**

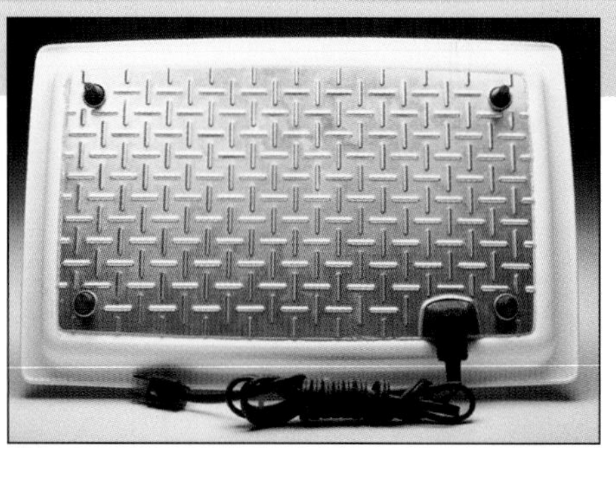

Blue Cornflower, tray, #P-54, Electromatic®, bottom view: showing metal bottom and cord; top view: identical to the #P-35, **$24.00.**

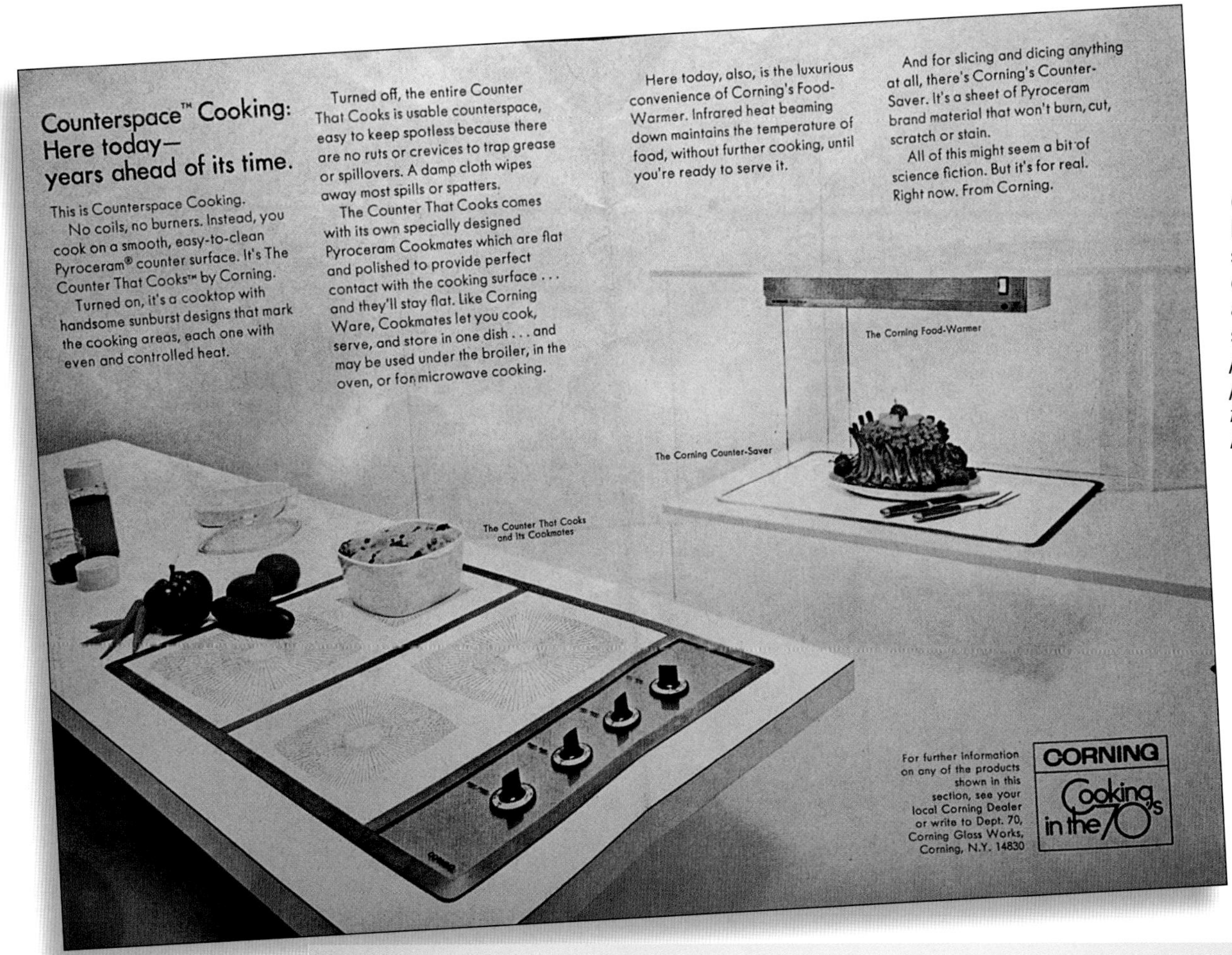

Corning brochure showing counter top and cooking surface. *Reprinted with permission from Corning Incorporated.*

Blue Cornflower, tray, warming, 1.5" tall, 17" long, 11" wide, electric, metal, no mark, **$12.50.** **Note**: This is a go along item since it was not made by Corning.

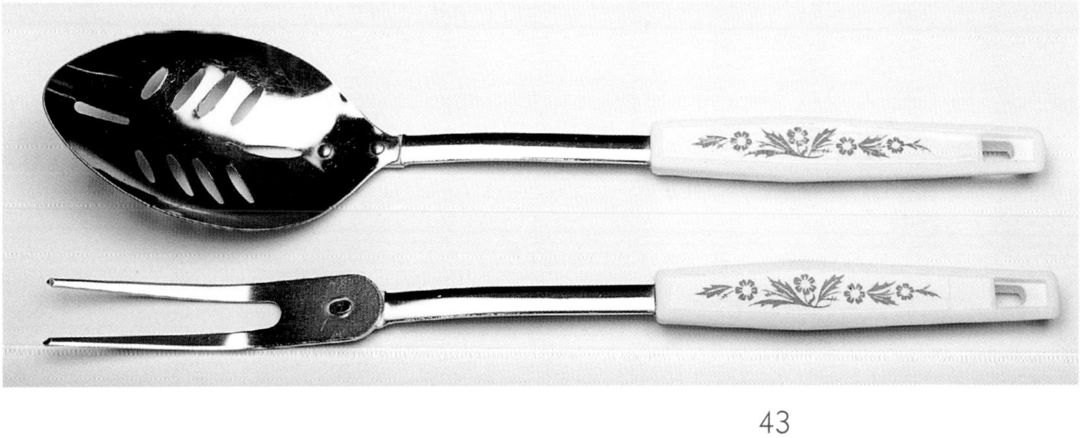

Blue Cornflower, serving utensils, chrome plated with white plastic handles and applied decal. **Left**: fork, 12" long; **right**: spoon with slots, 12" long, **$6.50 pair.** **Note**: This is a go along item since it was not made by Corning.

Blue Cornflower Go Along items. **Left:** Sugar shaker, 5.25" tall, chrome lid, clear with white fired on color and blue silk screen, embossed on bottom: Dispensers Inc., Santa Barbara, Calif. 7A 930, **$8.50**. **Center:** Shakers, 3.65" tall, 1.75" wide, Milk Glass with plastic silver tops marked S & P, marked on bottom 8828, **$6.50; right:** Syrup, 5.25" tall, chrome lid, clear with white fired on color and blue silk screen, embossed on bottom: Dispensers Inc., Santa Barbara, Calif. 7A 930, **$8.50. Note:** These are go along item since they were not made by Corning .

Blue Cornflower, Corelle®, bowl, 2.5" tall, 8.5" wide, serving, Corelle® dinner ware line, marked on the bottom: Corelle® by Corning Microwavable No broiler or stovetop, Made in USA, **$12.50.**

Blue Cornflower, piggy bank, 5" tall, 3.5" wide, 6.5" long, ceramic, marked on bottom: Made in England, **$29.50. Note:** This is a go along item since it was not made by Corning.

Platinum Starburst

The 1959 Corning catalog announced new additions to the Corning Ware® line. Besides, Corning now offering electric items, a new pattern was also introduced. Two new percolators were offered with a sleek platinum space-age design. The new pattern called Platinum Starburst was found only on the 6 cup and 8 cup percolators. It was obvious that the designers looked to the stars for an idea for this pattern. This bursting star reminds you of the inspirational star of Bethlehem. The Platinum Starburst was only offered on the percolators and by 1962 was discontinued. A Constellation casserole offered under the Pyrex® name in 1962 is very similar to this pattern.

Detail of Platinum Starburst pattern.

Platinum Starburst, coffee pot, 8 cup, 10.25" tall, 5" wide, marked on the side: 8 cup Corning Ware®, **$12.50**.

Platinum Starburst, detail of mark on side: 8 cup Corning Ware®.

Black Trefoil

Detail of Black Trefoil pattern.

The Black Trefoil pattern was introduced in 1960. This pattern must have been based on a space age idea. The design gives you the feeling of infinity that is so characteristic of the vastness of space. With the space exploration starting to heat up, we are sure Corning was looking to have a pattern that would appeal to a more sophisticated customer. Initially it was only offered on the Electromatic percolator. Next the Electromatic skillet was added in this pattern. Four other pieces can be found in this pattern. There were two non-electric percolators in the 6 and 9 cup size. Covered saucepans in the 1.75 quart and 2.5 quart sizes also could be purchased with cradles that had candle warmers in the bases. Desired customer sales didn't materialize and the pattern was discontinued in 1965.

Black Trefoil, casserole, covered, #P-1 ¾-B, 3.5" tall, 7.5" wide, 1.75 quart, marked on bottom Corning Ware®, lid marked with: P-7-C, **$9.50.**

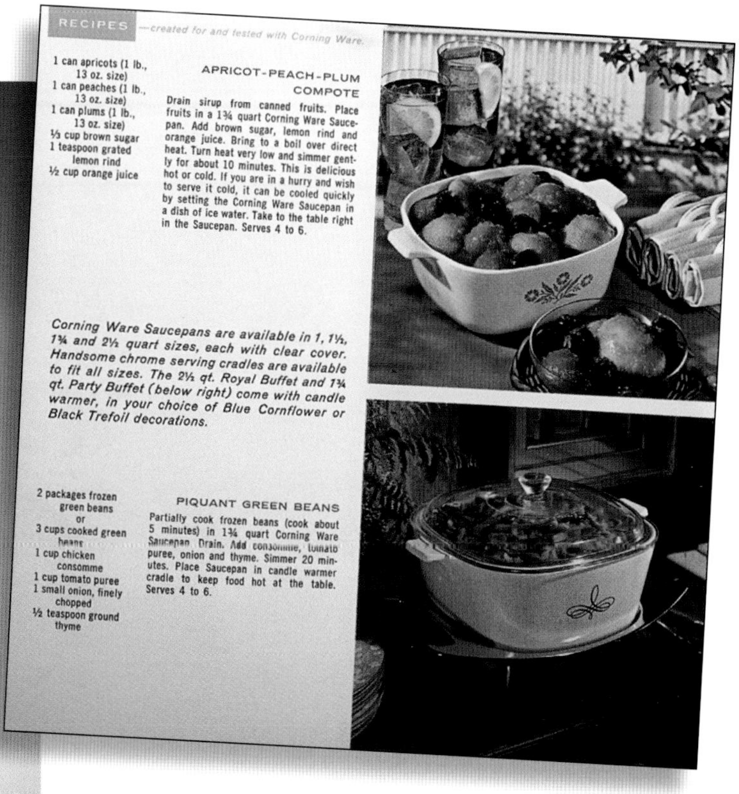

RECIPES —created for and tested with Corning Ware.

APRICOT-PEACH-PLUM COMPOTE

1 can apricots (1 lb., 13 oz. size)
1 can peaches (1 lb., 13 oz. size)
1 can plums (1 lb., 13 oz. size)
⅓ cup brown sugar
1 teaspoon grated lemon rind
½ cup orange juice

Drain sirup from canned fruits. Place fruits in a 1¾ quart Corning Ware Saucepan. Add brown sugar, lemon rind and orange juice. Bring to a boil over direct heat. Turn heat very low and simmer gently for about 10 minutes. This is delicious hot or cold. If you are in a hurry and wish to serve it cold, it can be cooled quickly by setting the Corning Ware Saucepan in a dish of ice water. Take to the table right in the Saucepan. Serves 4 to 6.

Corning Ware Saucepans are available in 1, 1½, 1¾ and 2½ quart sizes, each with clear cover. Handsome chrome serving cradles are available to fit all sizes. The 2½ qt. Royal Buffet and 1¾ qt. Party Buffet (below right) come with candle warmer, in your choice of Blue Cornflower or Black Trefoil decorations.

PIQUANT GREEN BEANS

2 packages frozen green beans
or
3 cups cooked green beans
1 cup chicken consomme
1 cup tomato puree
1 small onion, finely chopped
½ teaspoon ground thyme

Partially cook frozen beans (cook about 5 minutes) in 1¾ quart Corning Ware Saucepan. Drain. Add consomme, tomato puree, onion and thyme. Simmer 20 minutes. Place Saucepan in candle warmer cradle to keep food hot at the table. Serves 4 to 6.

Corning brochure featuring Cornflower and Black Trefoil. *Reprinted with permission from Corning Incorporated.*

Black Trefoil, Electromatic® percolator, #P-13-EP, 10" tall, 5" wide, 10 cup, marked on the side: Corning Ware®, black plastic trivet, 1" tall, 5" wide, 4 tab feet, marked in center: Corning Ware®, **$14.50.**

Top: Black Trefoil, skillet, covered, #P-10-B, 2" tall, 10.25" wide, not marked. **Bottom:** Electromatic skillet, white, #P-12-ES-N, 2" tall, 9.75" wide, **$24.50 set**. **Note:** We found when the skillet was sold with the Electromatic® skillet that it was not marked.

All White/ Just White

To appeal to a wider range of consumers, Corning began offering their cookware in plain white in 1965. This undecorated cookware was called, All White. These first pieces all had matching lids with black knobs and came in a variety of sizes. The line was expanded to include the percolators and a teapot. Consumers liked the plain white for its crisp, clean look. Many other pieces were offered with the line being renamed in 1977 to be Just White. Sales remained strong but in the early 1990s with so many new patterns were being offered, it was decided to discontinue the Just White line.

Heat and Eat, All White/ Just White, Grab It, Casser-ette, #P-150-B, 3" tall, 5.75" wide, 550ml, round, glass lid, marked on the handle: Grab It Range – Oven – Micro-wave Corning Ware® P-150-B 15 oz. 479 Corning, NY USA **$7.50**. **Note:** We also found pieces marked on the underside of the handle with: Corning Ware® P-150-B 550 ML 6 01.

Heat and Eat, All White/Just White, marked on the handle: Grab It Range – Oven – Microwave Corning Ware® P-150-B 15 oz. 479 Corning, NY USA.

All White/Just White, #P-140-B, 1" tall, 4.75" wide, 7" long, "Sidekick," small oval dish, marked on the bottom: Sidekick Corning Ware® P-140-B 4 ½ x 6 ¾ For oven and microwave Use caution in handling when hot Corning, NY, USA 479 MA, **$5.00**. **Back:** shown upright; **Front:** shown flat.

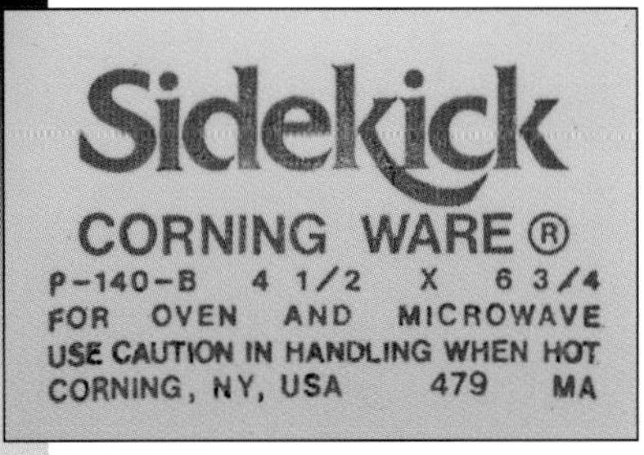

All White/Just White, #P-140-B, mark on bottom: Sidekick Corning Ware® P-140-B 4 ½ x 6 ¾ For oven and microwave Use caution in handling when hot Corning, NY, USA 479 MA.

All White/Just White, Heat and Eat, Casser-ette, #P-14-B, 2.5" tall, 6.5" long, 5.5" wide, 14 ounce, oval, glass lid, marked on the bottom: Corning Ware® P-14-B 14 ounce For Oven and Microwave Corning, NY USA 479 MA, **$8.50**.

All White/Just White, teapot with metal infuser, #P-104, 5" tall, 5.25" wide, 6 cup, marked on the side: Corning Ware® P-104 6 cup Corning, NY USA 1182MA, **$9.50.**

All White/ Just White, teapot, #TP-6, "Cookmates," 6.25" tall, 5.5" wide, 6 cup, marked on the side under the handle: Corning Ware® Cookmates TP-6, **$9.50.**

All White/Just White, Electromatic® percolator, #P-206-EP, 9" tall, 4.25" wide, 6 cup, marked on the bottom: Corning Ware® P-206-EP 6 cup Made in USA, **$12.50.**

All White/Just White, petite pan, #P-43-B, 2.25" tall, 5.25" wide, 700 ml, glass lid, marked on the bottom: Corning Ware® P-43-B 700ml Made in USA, **$9.50.**

All White/Just White, casserole, covered, #B-1, 2" tall, 7.75" wide, 1 quart, round, glass lid, marked on bottom: Corning Ware® Buffet Server B-1 Made in USA 1 qt., **$9.50**

All White/Just White, casserole, covered, #M-225-B, 3.75" tall, 8.25" wide, 2.3 liter, round with round tab handles, three raised crescent bars in bottom, marked on the underside of handles: on one side – Corning Ware® M-225-B 2.3 liter and on the other side – 6 16, **$8.50.**

All White/Just White, Buffet Server, casserole, covered, #B-2 ½, 5.75" tall, 8.75" wide, 2 ½ quart, round, black knob, marked on bottom: Corning Ware® Buffet Server B- 2 ½ Made in USA 2 ½ qt, **$12.50.**

All White/Just White, Buffet Server, detail of bottom mark.

All White/Just White, casserole, covered, #A-3-B, 3 liter, 3.75" tall, 8.5" wide, 3 quart, glass lid, marked on the underside of handles: Corning Ware® A-3-B 3 L USA, **$9.50.**

All White/Just White, browning fry pan, covered, #MW-83-B, 2" tall, 6.5" wide, long handle 3 tab feet, glass lid, marked on the underside of the handle: Corning Ware® MW-83-B Microwave Browning Dish, Maximum preheat at 4 minutes, Corning, NY, USA, 185 MA, **$7.50**.

All White/Just White, browning skillet, 2" tall, 8.5" wide, 1.5 quart, 4 tab feet, glass lid, marked on the bottom: Micromate Browner by Corning Made in USA, **$9.50**.

All White/Just White, marked on the bottom: Micromate Browner by Corning Made in USA.

All White/Just White, pie plate, #P-309, 1.5" tall, 9.75" wide, marked on the bottom: P-309 9 x 1 ¼ Corning Ware® For Range and Microwave USA, **$5.00**.

All White/Just White, baker, covered, #M-10-GR-B, 2" tall, 10.25" wide, 10 raised bars on the inside bottom, cradle with white plastic handles, marked on the underneath of one handle: Corning Ware® M-10-GR-B 10 inch cooker range-oven-microwave Corning, NY USA 178 MA, **$14.50.**

All White/Just White, pizza pan, #MW-12, 1.5" tall, 12" wide, marked on underside of handle: Corning Ware® MW-12 Microwave Crisper Do Not Cook on this Side Corning NY, USA 11181MA, **$8.50. Note:** There is special silver like surface on the underside that is designed to brown and make items crispy that is not to be cooked on directly.

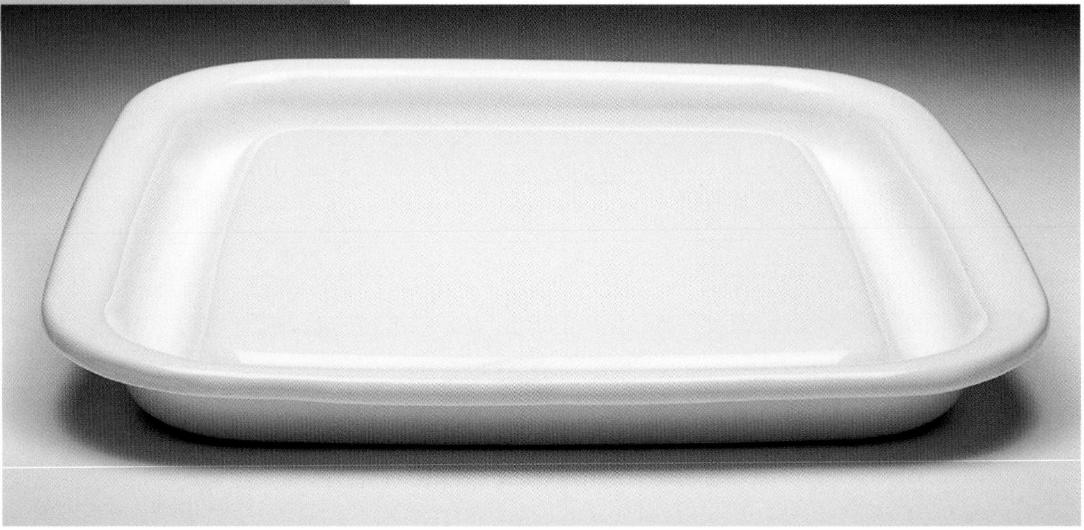

All White/Just White, browning tray, #MW-2, 12" long, 11.5" wide, marked on the underside lip: Corning Ware® MW-2 Microwave Browning Grill Do Not Cook on this Side Corning, NY USA 479 MA, **$7.50. Note:** There is a special silver like surface on the underside that is designed to brown, that is not to be cooked on directly.

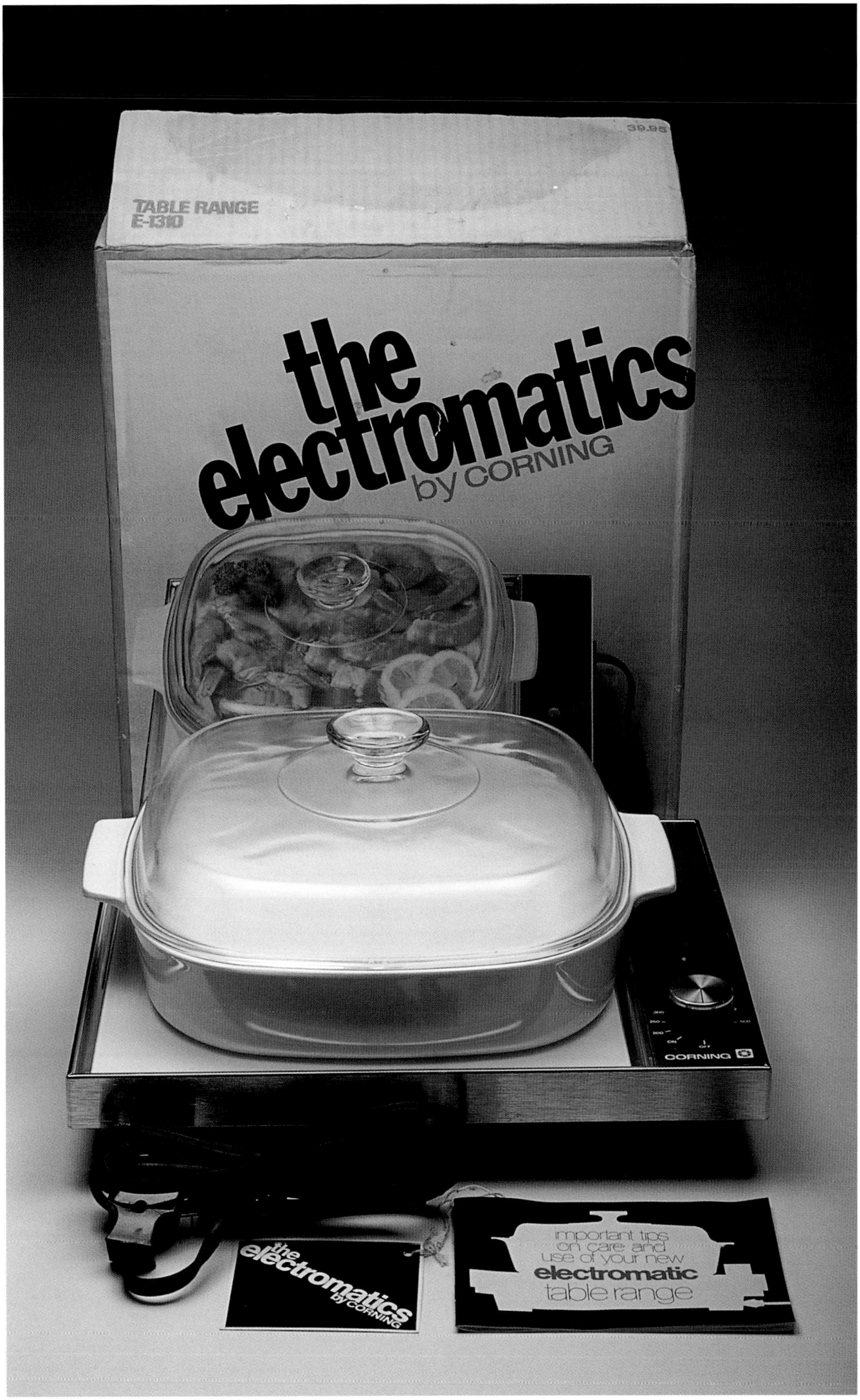

Table range, #E-1310. **Back:** original box. **Top:** All White, skillet, covered, #A-222-B, 2" tall, 10.25" wide; Bottom: Electromatic®, 2.5" tall, 11" wide, 13.5" long, glass-ceramic surface, metal frame, temperature gauge on side goes from 200° to 500° and signal light; **front:** original paper hang tag and brochure with operating instructions, cleaning information and recipes to use, **$19.50 set.**

Platinum Filigree

Detail of Platinum Filigree pattern.

The Platinum Filigree pattern was introduced in 1966. It was a small gift line with only four items. The pattern reminds you of a fancy silver ribbon on a gift package. The #P-420 1.75 quart covered saucepan was set in a cradle with a candle warmer and was called a Party Buffet. The #P-440 2.5 quart covered saucepan was also set in a cradle with candle warmer and this one was called a Royal Buffet. There were two Electromatic percolators; one was a 6 cup, #P-406-EP and the other a 10 cup, #P-480-EP. Both buffets were only offered for that first year while both sizes of percolators were continued until 1969.

Platinum Filigree, percolator, #P-480-EP, 10" tall, 5" wide, 10 cup, marked on the bottom: Corning Ware® P-480-EP 10 cup Made in USA, **$12.50.**

Detail of Platinum Filigree on bottom: Corning Ware® P-480-EP 10 cup Made in USA.

Avocado

The Avocado cookware had a solid green color on the outside of the bottom and a white lid with a green knob. This cookware was first offered in 1968 and continued until 1971. There were ten different pieces: three covered saucepans, two covered skillets, a Dutch oven, six-cup percolator, six-cup Electromatic percolator, nine-cup percolator and ten-cup Electromatic percolator. All the saucepans and skillets were all round. The percolators were all white with an avocado medallion design on them. The detachable handles for the saucepans and skillets were all white.

Detail of Avocado Medallion pattern.

Avocado Medallion, coffee pot, 10" tall, 5.5" wide, 9 cup, marked on side: Corning Ware® 9 cup, **$9.50**.

Avocado Medallion, detail of side mark: Corning Ware® 9 cup.

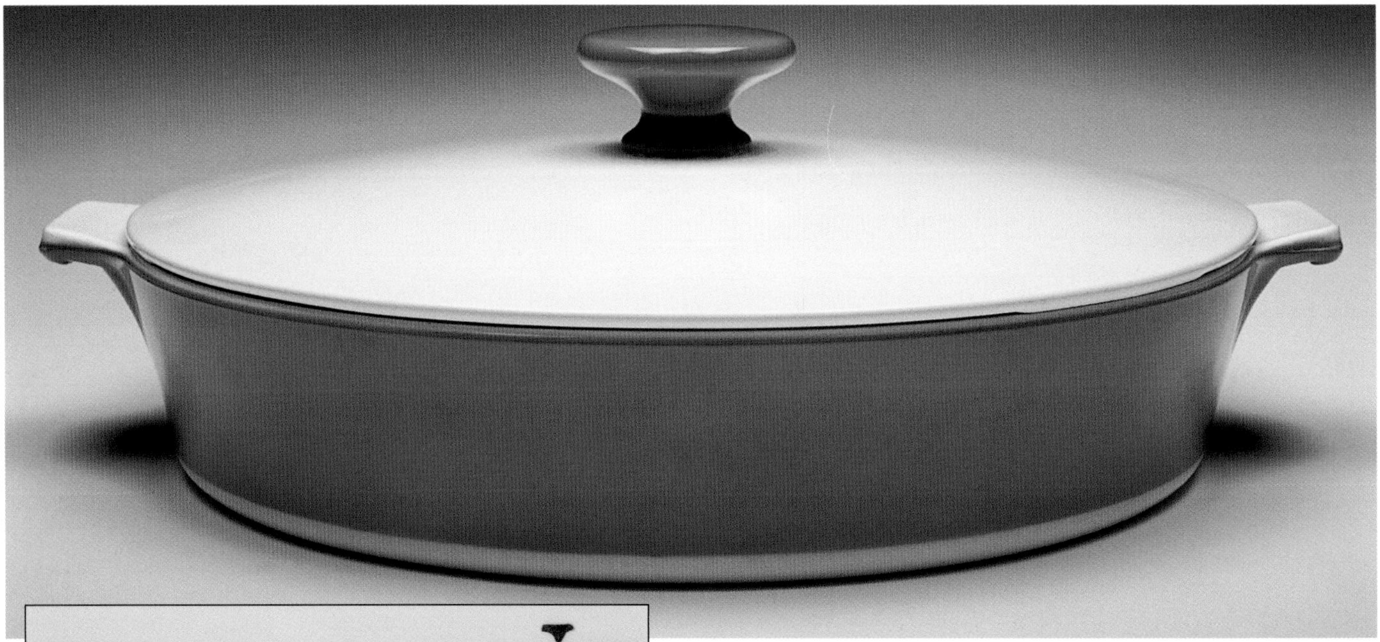

Avocado, detail of bottom mark: Corning Ware® Buffet Server Made in USA, 1 qt.

Avocado, casserole, covered, #B-1, 3.75" tall, 10.25" wide, 2 quart, marked on bottom: Corning Ware® Buffet Server Made in USA, 1 qt., **$9.50**.

Space-Age Cooking: a world of new ideas, new foods, new ways to cook and serve.

Space-age cooking is here. For you, it means more fun, less fuss—with ideas like convenience foods, boil-in-a-bag meals, international gourmet specialties your mother never dreamed of serving. In fact, today you can whip up a special meal for every member of the family in less time than it took her to cook one ordinary meal.

And, with new ideas like the electronic oven, infrared warming, Counterspace Cooking, and colorful Corning Ware® Cookware, you can be even more creative than ever—with less drudgery.

The one type of cookware that's ideal for all kinds of space-age cooking is Corning Ware, the only cookware that's made from Pyroceram® glass ceramic—the unique material that was born for the space-age and is still keeping pace with it.

Because it can withstand extreme changes in heat and cold without breaking or warping, Corning Ware is guaranteed never to break from temperature extremes and is ideal for every type of cooking . . . including microwave ovens, where metal is not recommended.

Choice? Corning Ware keeps its lead in the 70's with more than 80 different pieces for every cooking need, many in the exciting new Avocado and Butterscotch colors.

Corning welcomes you to "Cooking in the 70's" . . . with the cookware for the 70's and for today —Corning Ware Cookware, perfect to own . . . perfect to give.

Corning Ware Butterscotch Set: 1, 1¾ qt. covered saucepans, 8½ in. covered skillet and white detachable handle, $24.95

Corning Ware Avocado Set: 1, 1¾ qt. covered saucepans, 8½ in. covered skillet and white detachable handle, $24.95

Corning promises to replace any Corning Ware product that ever breaks from temperature extremes. Just return the pieces to a Corning Ware Products Dealer.

CORNING
Cooking in the 70's

Corning Brochure: cooking in the '70s. *Reprinted with permission from Corning Incorporated.*

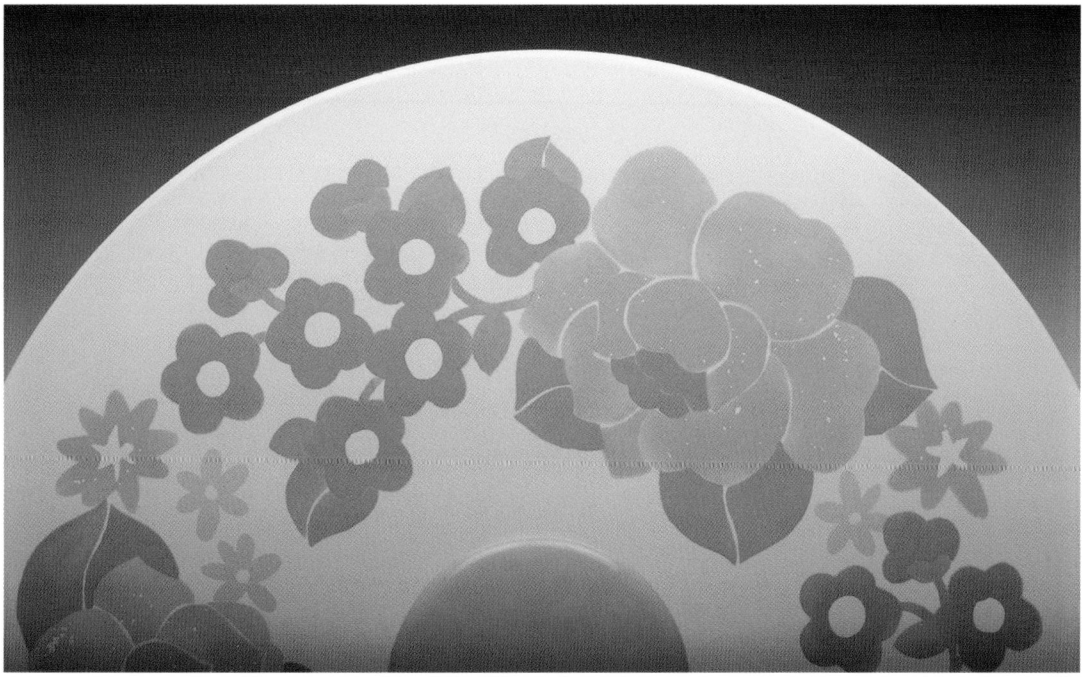

Butterscotch/ Summerhill

Detail of Butterscotch/ Summerhill pattern.

The Butterscotch color was introduced in 1969 and discontinued a short time later in 1970. It was advertised as being a mellow harvest gold that blends in with your other colors. This color reminds you of the butterscotch candy. The round Butterscotch cookware had a yellow-orange solid color on the outside of the bottom and had a white lid with a coordinating knob. The colored knob was attached with a textured metal peg that was inserted into the lid. We have found that many of these knobs have loosened and there is no way to tighten them. This causes the lids to be very wobbly when picked up, which makes them not very useful.

When there was a floral decoration on the lid, it was called Summerhill. The ten different pieces in this line were: three covered saucepans, two covered skillets and a Dutch oven. The detachable handles for the saucepans and skillets were all white. For some odd reason there were no percolators made in this color.

Butterscotch/Summerhill. **Left**: #B-1¾-B, casserole, covered, 3" tall, 8" wide, 1.75 quart, round, marked on bottom: Corning Ware® B-1 ¾-B 1 ¾ qt., MADE IN USA, **$9.50; right**: #B-2 ½ -B, casserole, covered, 3.25" tall, 9" wide, 2.5 quart, round, marked on bottom: Corning Ware® B-21/2-B 2 ½ qt, MADE IN USA, **$12.50.**

Butterscotch/Summerhill, Casserole, covered, #B-1, 2" tall, 7.75" wide, 1 quart, round, white lid and knob with gold flowers, gold base, marked on bottom: Centura® by Corning 1 qt. saucepan, **$12.50.**

Butterscotch/Summerhill, mark on bottom: Centura® by Corning 1 qt. saucepan.

Renaissance

Detail of Renaissance pattern. *Photo courtesy of Replacements, Ltd.*

Renaissance was to be the first of a limited edition gift line. It was only made in 1970. The description in the catalog listed the cookware as modern shapes set with a 17th century etching. The setting was a Swedish seaport showing the architecture, types of transportation and street scenes of the time period. A special gray color was used to imitate the etching as it would appear on white paper. As an added appeal to this cookware, beautifully designed shipping boxes matched the scene on the item. There were only five items in this pattern. There were a nine-cup percolator, 1.75 quart party buffet saucepan, 2.5 quart royal buffet saucepan, a 4 quart covered saucepan set in a cradle and a serving tray in a cradle. This pattern is extremely hard to find today so it may have been limited to select areas. Our guess is that the consumer probably liked it but it didn't fit into most kitchens.

Renaissance, P-84, 4" tall, 10.25" wide, 4 quart, glass lid, marked, **$45.00**. *Photo courtesy of Replacements, Ltd.*

Nature's Bounty

Detail of the Nature's Bounty pattern.

Nature's Bounty was another limited edition cookware line that Corning tried only in 1971. Gold colored vegetables made up the decoration. There were six items in this line, including a 1.75 quart party buffet saucepan, a 2.5 quart royal buffet saucepan, a 4 quart covered saucepan set in a cradle, a 10 inch covered skillet set in a cradle, a loaf pan with a plastic lid, and an 8-cup percolator.

Nature's Bounty, casserole, covered, #P-84-B, 4" tall, 10.25" wide, 4 quart, glass lid, metal cradle with wood handles – 8.5" wide, 13.5" long, marked on the bottom: Corning Ware® P-84-B Made in USA for range & microwave, **$19.50.**

Merry Mushroom

Merry Mushroom was issued in 1971. This pattern featured an attractive grouping of different colors of mushrooms. The spotted mushroom has two fern fronds on each side of it. There were four covered saucepans, a teapot, and a beverage server made in this pattern.

This pattern was coordinated to go with Sears's extensive line of ceramic items that matched the cookware.

Merry Mushroom, casserole, B-1-B, #2.25" tall, 7.75" wide, 1 quart, marked on bottom, **$14.50.** *Photo courtesy of Replacements, Ltd.*

Harvest Gold

Harvest Gold was a variation of the earlier issued Butterscotch pattern. This was only offered in 1971 as a three piece set, item #P-33-6. There were 1, 1.5 and 1.75 quart saucepans each offered with clear glass lids. These plain gold items could easily coordinate with the Floral Bouquet pattern.

Harvest Gold, casserole, covered, #P-1 ¾-B, 3.5" tall, 7.5" wide, 1.75 quart, clear glass lid with colored knob, marked, **$9.50.** *Photo courtesy of Replacements, Ltd.*

Lancaster

Detail of Lancaster pattern.

The Lancaster pattern was only offered on a teapot. Various different patterns were offered on the 6 cup teapot as a promotional item in 1971 only.

Lancaster, teapot, #P-104, 5" tall, 5.25" wide, 6 cup, marked on the side: Corning Ware® 6 cup, **$12.50.**

Floral Bouquet

Detail of large flowers on Floral Bouquet pattern.

In 1971, Floral Bouquet was the first full line of cookware offered since the introduction of Cornflower. This cookware was advertised as the convenience that bloomed in the kitchen since the flowers wouldn't wilt in either the hot or cold. There are slightly different versions of the flowers depending on the item. The first pieces had a full detailed pattern that continued around the entire piece. The pattern was restyled to portray just a small grouping of flowers set against the white background. Floral Bouquet was discontinued in 1974.

Floral Bouquet, casserole, covered, #P-1 ¾-B, 3.5" tall, 7.5" wide, 1.75 quart, glass lid, marked on bottom: Corning Ware® P-1 ¾-B 1 ¾ quart MADE IN USA, **$9.50.**

Floral Bouquet, skillet, covered, #P-10-B, 2" tall, 10.25" wide, 2.5 quart, glass lid, **$12.50.**

Floral Bouquet, percolator, #P-219-B, 9 cup, 10.5" tall, 5.25" wide, marked on the bottom: Corning Ware® P-219-B 9 cup Made in USA, **$12.50.**

Detail of small flowers on Floral Bouquet pattern.

Floral Bouquet, petite pan, covered, #P-43-B, 2.25" tall, 5.25" wide, 2.75 cups, glass lid, marked on the bottom: Corning Ware® P-43-B 2 ¾ cup Made in USA for Range & Microwave, **$9.50**.

Floral Bouquet, casserole, covered, #P-1-B, 2" tall, 7.25" wide, 1 quart, glass lid, marked on bottom: Corning Ware® P-1-B 1 qt. Made in USA For Range & Microwave, **$7.50**.

Floral Bouquet, casserole, covered, #A-1-B, 2" tall, 7" wide, 1 quart, glass lid, marked on bottom: A-1-B 1 quart Corning Ware® for Range and Microwave USA, **$7.50.**

Floral Bouquet, casseroles, glass lid, covered, to show size difference. **Left:** #P-2 ½ -B, 2.5 quart, **$12.50; right:** #P-43-B, 2.75 cups, **$9.50.**

Floral Bouquet, casserole, covered, #P-2 ½ -B, 3.75" tall, 8.25" wide, 2 ½ quart, glass lid, marked on the bottom: Corning Ware® P-2 ½ -B 2 ½ quart Made in USA For Range & Microwave, **$12.50.**

Floral Bouquet, mark on bottom: Corning Ware® P-2 ½ -B 2 ½ quart Made in USA For Range & Microwave.

Floral Bouquet, saucepan, covered, #P-81-B, 2″ tall, 6″ wide, 1 pint, glass lid, marked on the bottom: P-81-B 1 pint Corning Ware® for range and microwave USA, **$7.50.**

Floral Bouquet, skillet, covered, #P-83-B, 1.5″ tall, 6.5″ wide, glass lid marked on the bottom: Corning Ware® P-83-B 6 ½ in Made in USA For range & microwave, **$8.50**.

Floral Bouquet, Dutch oven, covered, #P-34-B, 4″ tall, 11.5″ wide, 12.25″ long, 5 quarts, glass lid, inner wire rack, marked under the lip: Corning Ware® Dutch Oven P-34-B Made in USA 5 quart, **$22.50.**

Floral Bouquet, tri-corner sauce pan, covered, #P-55-B, 6" tall, 7.25" wide, 1 quart, glass lid, detachable handle, marked on side: Corning Ware®, P-55-B MADE IN USA FOR RANGE & MICROWAVE, **$19.50**.

Floral Bouquet, percolator, electric, #P-6-EP, 9.25" tall, 4.5" wide, 6 cup, marked on side: Corning Ware® 6 cup, **$12.50.**

Spice O' Life

Detail of "Le Thé" on the Spice O' Life.

Spice O' Life was introduced in 1972 and was the first new pattern offered on the redesigned cookware. The walls were made thinner and straighter. The tab handles were made larger. The bottom now was flatter so it set down better against the cooking surface. The lids fit tighter and also had larger knobs on them for ease in picking them up. Herbs and spices mixed with vegetables created a distinctive French look about it. Various French words were used on different pieces. The following definitions are given for the French words. Le Persil= Parsley; La Sauge= Sage; L'Echalote= Shallot; La Marjolaine= Marjoram; Le Romarin= Rosemary; LeCafe= Coffee; Le The= Tea.

The first year the Spice O' Life was offered there were 14 items and through the years the number of items would greatly increase. After its first year on the market this pattern was described as offering a year of seasoning since it had gained such acceptance by the consumer. Spice O' Life would remain one of the most popular cookware lines ever offered by Corning. This pattern was discontinued in 1988 after 16 years of serving meals to America's favorite families.

Spice O' Life casserole and cutting board with lobster chef holding vegetables.

Spice O' Life, sauce pan, covered, #P-150-B, 2" tall, 5.5" wide, 1.25 pint, glass lid, round tab handle, marked on handle: Corning Ware® P-150-B, **$8.50.**

Spice O' Life, teapot, #P-104, 5" tall, 6" wide, 6 cup, "Le Thé" marked on the side: Corning Ware® 6 cup P-104, **$9.50.**

Spice O' Life, saucepan with glass lid, #B-1-B, 2.25" tall, 7.75" wide, 1 quart, round, "L'Echalote," 10 recessed circles on glass lid, marked on the bottom: B-1-B 1 Quart Corning Ware® For Range and Microwave USA, **$7.50.**

Spice O' Life, detail of mark on bottom: #P-4-B 7x5 1/2x3 inch Range-Oven-Microwave Corning, NY USA 1181 MA.

Spice O' Life, saucepan with lid, #P-4-B, 3.5" tall, 6" wide, 7.5" long, glass lid, rectangle, "Le Persil La Sauge," marked on the bottom: #P-4-B 7x5 1/2x3 inch Range-Oven-Microwave Corning, NY USA 1181 MA, **$11.50**.

Spice O' Life, loaf pan, #P-315-B, 3.25" tall, 5.4" wide, 10.75" long, "La Marjolaine," marked on bottom: P-315-B 9x5x3 Corning Ware® For Range and Microwave USA, **$9.50.**

Spice O' Life, baker, covered, #MC-1-B, 3" tall, 6.75" wide, 8.75" long, 4 tab feet, marked on bottom: Corning Ware® MC-1B 7x5 1/2x2 inch For oven and microwave Corning, NY USA 179 MA, glass lid has 5 rows of 7 each of indented circles, marked on edge with Pyrex® MC-1-C, **$9.50.**

Spice O' Life, baker, square, #P-322, 2.5" tall, 8.75" wide, "L'Echalote," marked on the bottom: Corning Ware® P-322 8x8x2 inch Range Oven Microwave Corning NY USA 178MA, **$12.50.**

Spice O' Life, roaster, open, A-18, 2.5" tall, 9.75" wide, 12" long, metal rack for roasting and lifting out, marked on the underside of rim: Corning Ware® A-18 10 ¼ x 8 ½ x 2 ¼ inch Range-Oven – Microwave Corning, NY USA 479 MA, **$14.50.**

Spice O' Life, mark on bottom: Corning Ware® A-18 10 ¼ x 8 ½ x 2 ¼ inch Range-Oven – Microwave Corning, NY USA 479 MA.

Spice O' Life, roaster, open, #P-332, 2" tall, 8.75" wide, 13.25" long, marked on the bottom: P-332 12x7 1/2x2 Corning Ware® For range and Microwave USA, **$12.50**.

Spice O' Life, roaster, open, #A-21, 2.5" tall, 11.5" wide, 14.5" long, "Le Romarin," marked on the bottom: A-21 12 ¼ x 10 ¼ x 2 ¼ For range and microwave USA, **$13.50.**

Spice O' Life, detail of "La Sauge" on Spice O' Life.

Spice O' Life, spouted sauce pan, covered, #P-89-B, 2.5" tall, 6.5" wide, 2.5 cup, "La Sauge," long handle, glass lid, marked on bottom: Corning Ware® P-89-B 2 ½ cup Range – Oven – Microwave Corning, NY, USA 184 MA; it was also embossed on the bottom with: Corning Ware® P-82-B 750mL, **$8.50.**

Spice O' Life, saucepan with lid, #P-32-B, 2.5" tall, 6" wide, 1.5 pint, glass lid, long handle, "La Marjolaine," marked on the bottom: Corning Ware® P-32-B 1 ½ pint Range-Oven-Microwave Corning, NY USA 379 MA, **$8.50**.

Spice O' Life, detail of mark on the bottom: Corning Ware® P-32-B 1 ½ pint Range-Oven-Microwave Corning, NY USA 379 MA, **$7.50**. **Note:** This is the only time we found a piece of this pattern marked on the bottom in blue.

Spice O' Life, petite pans. **Left:** #P-43-B Corning 2.25" tall, 5.25" wide, 2 ¾ cup, glass lid, marked on bottom: Corning Ware® P-43-B 2 ¾ cup Range Oven Microwave Corning, NY USA 477MA, **$9.50; right:** #P-41-B, 1.5" tall, 5.25" wide, 1 ¾ cup, plastic lid, marked on bottom: P-41-B 1 ¾ cup Corning Ware® For range and microwave USA, **$6.50.**

Spice O' Life, covered, glass lid. **Left**: saucepan, #P-81-B, 2" tall, 6" wide, 1 pint, marked on bottom: P-81-B 1 pint, Corning Ware® For range and microwave USA; **$8.50; right**: skillet, #P-83-B, 2" tall, 7" wide, 1.25 pint, marked on bottom: P-83-B 6 ½ inch Corning Ware® for range and microwave USA, **$8.50.**

Spice O' Life, detail of "L'Echalote" on Spice O' Life.

Spice O' Life, skillets with glass lids. **Left**: #A-1-B, 2" tall, 7" wide, 1 quart, "L'Echalot" marked on the underside of handle: Corning Ware® A-1-B 1 quart Range-Oven-Microwave Corning, NY USA 179 MA, **$8.50; right**: A-8-B, 2" tall, 8.5" wide, 1.5 quart, "L'Echalot," marked on the underside of handle: 8x8x1 ¾ inch Range-Oven-Microwave Corning, NY USA 11182 MA, **$9.50.**

Spice O' Life, detail of "Le Persil La Sauge" on Spice O' Life.

Spice O' Life, saucepan with glass lid, #A-1 ½-B, 2.75" tall, 7" wide, 1.5 quart, "Le Persil La Sauge," marked on the underside of the handle: Corning Ware® A-1 ½-B 1 ½ Quart Range-Oven-Microwave Corning, NY USA 179 MA, **$8.50**.

Spice O' Life, detail of mark on underside of handle: Corning Ware® A-1 ½-B 1 ½ Quart Range-Oven-Microwave Corning, NY USA 179 MA.

Spice O' Life, detail of "La Marjolaine" in Spice O' Life.

Spice O' Life, casserole, covered, #A-2-B, 2.5" tall, 8.5" wide, 2 quart, "La Marjolaine" glass lid, marked on the underside of one handle: Corning Ware® A-2-B 2 QT Range Oven Microwave Corning NY USA 278MA, **$9.50.**

Spice O' Life, detail of "L'Echalote La Marjolaine" on Spice O' Life.

Spice O' Life, casserole, covered, #A-3-B, 3.75" tall, 8.5" tall, 3 quart, glass lid, "L'Echalote La Marjolaine," wide handles, marked on the bottom: A-3-B 3 quart Corning Ware® For range and microwave USA, **$14.50**. **Note:** The 3 liter measures exactly the same, but it is, instead, marked underneath the handles with the following: Corning Ware® on one side and A-3-B 3 liter on the other one.

Spice O' Life, detail of "L'Echalote
La Marjolaine Le Romarin" on
Spice O' Life.

Spice O' Life, casserole, covered, #A-5-B, 4.25" tall, 10.25" wide, 5 quart, "L'Echalote La Marjolaine Le Romarin" glass lid, marked on the underside of one handle: Corning Ware® A-5-B 5 quart Range Oven Microwave Corning, NY USA 11182MA, **$22.50**.

Spice O' Life, detail of "Le Romarin" on Spice O' Life.

Spice O' Life, skillet with glass lid, #A-10-B, 2.15" tall, 10.25" wide, 2.25 quarts, "Le Romarin," metal cradle, marked on the bottom: A-10-B 9 3/4x 9 ¾ x 2 Corning Ware® For Range and Oven USA, **$13.50.**

Spice O' Life, RangeToppers™ sauce pans, glass lids.
Left: #N-2 ½-B, 4" tall, 8" wide, 2 ½ quart, marked on the side: RangeToppers™ N-2 ½-B 2 ½ Quart Not for microwave use Corning, NY USA 180 MA, **$29.50;**
right: #N – 1 ½-B, 3.25" tall, 7" wide, 1.5 quart, marked on side: Range Toppers™ N-1 ½-B 1 ½ Quart Not for microwave use Corning, NY USA 379 MA, **$24.50.**

IMPORTANT TIPS ON STORING
CORNING WARE®
RANGETOPPERS™
cookware

DO NOT nest Rangetoppers cookware when storing. Contact between the handle and one of the vessels below can damage the cookware and result in breakage. Chipped or cracked ware should not be used.

WE RECOMMEND storing each Rangetoppers cookware item separately. If storage space does not permit this, we suggest storing the cookware as illustrated below.

Invert the clear glass cover for each item and place on the appropriate saucepan/skillet. Then stack by size, largest on bottom.

Note:
If you must nest the vessels, place a cloth between them to prevent glass-to-glass contact.

SAVE THESE INSTRUCTIONS WITH YOUR USE & CARE BOOKLET

CORNING

LC-832 Supp. 1/80 MA

Printed in U.S.A.

Spice O' Life brochure of RangeToppers™. *Reprinted with permission from Corning Incorporated.*

GUARANTEE

Corning Glass Works, Corning, New York, unconditionally guarantees that any CORNING WARE® Products Dealer is authorized to replace, upon return of the broken pieces, any CORNING WARE Dish that ever breaks from temperature extremes.

"CORNING WARE," "PYREX" and "PYROCERAM" are registered trademarks of

CORNING GLASS WORKS, CORNING, N.Y. 14830

Printed in U.S.A.

LC-368A

Spice O' Life, brochure, "Use & Care of Corning Ware® Cookware" – Guarantee. *Reprinted with permission from Corning Incorporated.*

Spice O' Life, detail of mark on the side: RangeToppers™ N-2 ½-B 2 ½ Quart Not for microwave use Corning, NY USA 180 MA.

Spice O' Life, RangeToppers™ sauce pan, #N-2 ½-B, upside down to show metal bottom, **$24.50 w/o lid.**

Spice O' Life, RangeToppers™ fry pans, glass lids. **Top:** #N-8 ½-B, 2" tall, 8.75" wide, 1.5 quart, marked on the side: RangeToppers™ N-8 -½-B 8 ½ inch Not For Microwave Use Corning, NY USA 180MA, **$24.50; bottom:** #N-10-B, 2" tall, 10.25" wide, 2.25 quart, marked on the side: RangeToppers™ N-10-B 10 inch Not For Microwave Use Corning, NY USA 180MA, **$29.50.**

Spice O' Life, detail of mark on the side: RangeToppers™ N-10-B 10 inch Not For Microwave Use Corning, NY USA 180MA.

Spice O' Life, RangeToppers™ sauce pan, #N-5-B, 5.25" tall, 10.5" wide, 5 quart, glass lid, marked on the underside of handle: RangeToppers™ N-5-B 5 Quart Not for Microwave Use Corning, NY USA 180 MA, **$39.50.**

Spice O' Life, RangeToppers™ sauce pan, #N-5-B, upside to show metal bottom.

Spice O' Life, cutting board, 15" long, 11" wide, marked on the front: "LaSauge," four tab feet, **$9.50. Note:** This is made of Pyroceram® and was an accessory item.

Spice O' Life, storage jar, 7.5" tall, 6.25" wide, glass with plastic lid, #7080-G, marked on bottom edge with: Pyrex® Made in USA Not for freezer or range top use, **$6.00. Note:** This is a go along item since it was made by Corning out of Pyrex glass and not Pyroceram®.

Spice O' Life, domed cheese and cracker server, 5.75" tall, 10" wide, 12.5" long**, $8.50. Note:** This is a go along item since it was not made by Corning.

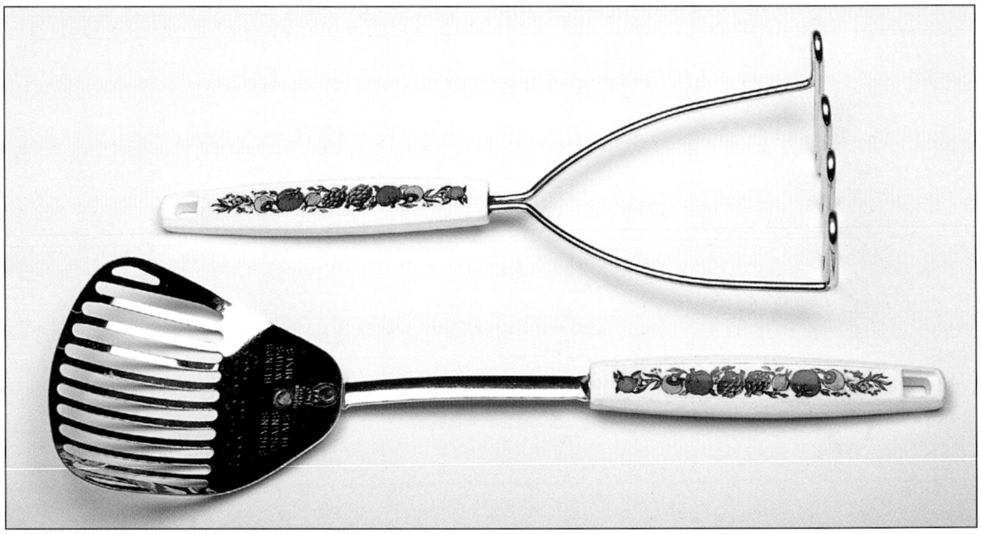

Spice O' Life, utensils, Chrome with plastic handles. **Left:** Potato masher, 10" long, **$3.50; right:** Whipper, 12.5" long, marked on the front: Kitchamajig, Strains Drains Beats Blends Whips Mixes Chromium Plated Ekco USA, **$3.50. Note:** This is a go along item since it was not made by Corning.

Country Festival

Detail of Country Festival pattern.

When Country Festival was introduced in 1975 it was advertised as offering a feeling back to the days of cooking over the open fire. It obviously has a Pennsylvania Dutch flair or folk art feel to it. For some reason, this pattern has been given the incorrect name among collectors. When searching on line for prices, we frequently found this pattern called Friendship. We also found that this was the only Corning pattern to have a date and Corning listed underneath the pattern. Country Festival was only offered until 1976.

Detail of Country Festival, with close up of the date of 1975 and Corning.

Country Festival, casserole, covered, #P-4-B, 3.25" tall, 7.5" long, 6" wide, rectangle shape, glass lid, marked on bottom: P-4-B 7 x 5 ½ x 3 Corning Ware® For Range and Microwave U. S. A., **$11.50.**

Country Festival, casserole, covered, #A-1, 2" tall, 7.25" wide, 1 quart, glass lid, marked on bottom: A-1 1 quart Corning Ware® For range and microwave USA, **$7.50.**

Country Festival, casserole, covered, glass lid. **Left**: #A-1 ½ -B, 2.75" tall, 7" wide, 1.5 quart, marked on the bottom: A-1 ½ -B 1 quart Corning Ware® for range and microwave USA, **$9.50; right**: #P-41-B, 1.5" tall, 5.25" wide, 1.75 cup, marked on the bottom: #P-41-B 1 ¾ cup Corning Ware® for range and microwave USA, **$8.50.**

Country Festival, skillet, covered, #A-8-B, 2" tall, 8.5" wide, glass lid, marked on the bottom: A-8-B 8x8x1 ¾ Corning Ware® For range and microwave USA, **$9.50**.

Country Festival, casserole, covered, #A-2-B, 2.5" tall, 8.5" wide, 2 quart, glass lid, marked on the bottom: A-2-B 2 quart Corning Ware® for range and microwave USA, **$9.50.**

Country Festival. **Top right:** sauce pan, covered, #P-81-B, 2" tall, 5.75" wide, 1 pint, glass lid, marked on bottom: #P-81-B 1 pint Corning Ware® For Range and Microwave USA, **$7.50; bottom left**: fry pan, covered, #P-83-B, 1.75" tall, 6.75" wide, 1.25 pint, glass lid, marked on bottom: #P-83-B 6 ½ inch Corning Ware® for Range and Microwave USA, **$8.50.**

Blue Heather

Detail of Blue Heather pattern.

Blue Heather was one of the short lived designer patterns from the late 1970s. Only a 1.5 quart covered casserole and a 2.5 quart covered casserole along with a tea pot were made. The pattern really resembles the heather flower. There was also a Heather Corelle® dinnerware line. The pieces were last listed in the Corning Glass Works newsletter in 1979.

Blue Heather, teapot, #P-104, 5.25" tall, 6" wide, 6 cup, marked on the side: Corning Ware® 6 cup P-104, **$12.50.**

Indian Summer

Detail of Indian Summer pattern.

Indian Summer was another of the designer patterns from the late 1970s that was only made for a short period of time. Two covered casseroles, a 1.5 quart and a 2.5 quart were made together with a teapot. A Corelle dinnerware line in Indian Summer was also made. By 1979, the pattern was discontinued.

Meadow

Meadow was a wonderful combination of wildflowers that could be found in a meadow. Just visualize being out for a walk in a field and seeing all of these beautiful flowers. This was one of the designer patterns that were only offered in 1976 and 1977. Besides the teapot, there were also only two covered casseroles that were made.

Meadow, teapot, 5.25" tall, 6 cup, **$9.50**.

Wildflower

Detail of the Wild Flower pattern.

A few short years after Spice O' Life, was offered, Corning introduced a new pattern called Wildflower in1977. This would soon prove to be another major pattern that was extremely popular with the consumer. An ad in the *Women's Day* described the Wildflower as a summery flower that would match any kitchen color scheme. Any recipe in the Wildflower turns into a feast for the eyes. Initially there were 5 covered saucepans, a skillet, 2 open roasters, petite pan, 2 menu-ette pans, and a teapot. This was the first new pattern to be offered in a Trio Set Special. Later, new patterns would be introduced in this boxed combination. The set contained a 1 quart and 1.5 quart covered saucepan with plastic and glass lids and a 2 quart glass-covered saucepan. Wildflower pieces were also offered as a RangeTopper. After the RangeTopper was introduced, Corning began to change their terminology on their pans. The RangeToppers were now the saucepans for the range. The formerly titled saucepans were now renamed to be covered casseroles and the skillets were called shallow casseroles. Wildflower was also made in the Corelle® dinnerware line. This pattern remained popular until it was discontinued in 1985.

Wildflower, casserole, covered, #P-4-B, 3.25″ tall, 7.25″ long, 6.25″ wide, rectangle, glass lid, marked on bottom: Corning Ware® P-4-B 7x5 1/2x3 inch Range Oven Microwave Corning, NY USA 479MA, **$11.50.**

Wildflower, detail of bottom mark: Corning Ware® P-4-B 7x5 1/2x3 inch Range Oven Microwave Corning, NY USA 479MA.

Wild Flower. **Left**: Square baking pan, #P-322, 2.5″ tall, 9″ wide, 9.75″ wide with flared edge, marked on bottom: Corning Ware® P-322 8x8x2 inch Range-Oven-Microwave Corning, NY, USA 1183MA, **$12.50; Right**: Casserole, covered, #A-3-B, 3.75″ tall, 9″ wide, 3 quart, glass lid, marked underneath handles: Corning Ware® A-3-B 3 quart Range – Oven – Microwave Corning, NY, USA 182MA, **$14.50.**

Wild Flower, petite pan, #P-43-B, 2.25" tall, 5.25" wide, 2.75 cup, plastic lid, marked on the bottom: Corning Ware® P-43-B 2 ¾ cup Range – Oven – Microwave Corning, NY USA 376MA, **$7.50.**

Wild Flower, petite pan, #P-43-B, 2.25" tall, 5.25" wide, 2.75 cup, glass lid, marked on the bottom: Corning Ware® P-43-B 2 ¾ cup Range – Oven – Microwave Corning, NY USA 376MA, **$9.50.**

Wild Flower, skillet with glass lid, #A-1-B, 2" tall, 7" wide, marked on the bottom: A-1-B 1 quart Corning Ware® For range and Microwave USA, **$8.50.**

Wildflower, casserole, covered, #A-2-B, 1.75 quart, 2" tall, 8.5" tall, 2 quart, glass lid, marked on handles: A-2-B 2 liter and Corning Ware®, **$9.50**.

Wildflower, casserole, covered, #A-10-B, 2.2" tall, 10.25"wide, 2.5 liter, glass lid, marked on the underside of one of the handles: Corning Ware® A-10-B, 10x10x2 inch, Range-Oven-Microwave, Corning, NY, USA 182 MA, **$12.50**. **Note**: This piece was also found to be marked with: A-10-B 2.5 liter.

Wildflower, mark on the underside of handle: Corning Ware® A-10-B, 10x10x2 inch, Range-Oven-Microwave, Corning, NY, USA 182 MA.

Wildflower, sauce pan, covered, #P-81-B, 1 pint, 2" tall, 6" wide, glass lid, marked on bottom: Corning Ware® P-81-B 1 pint, Range – oven-microwave Corning, NY. USA 179 MA; marked on lid: Pyrex® P-81-C, **$7.50.**

Wild Flower, fry pan, #N -8 ½-B, 2.25" tall, 9" wide, upside down to show metal, marked on edge under the handle: RangeToppers™, N -8 ½-B 8 ½ inch Not for microwave use Corning NY USA 180MA, **$20.00.**

Wild Flower, RangeToppers™, sauce pan, covered, #N-1 ½ -B, 3.5" tall, 6.75" wide, 1.5 quart, glass lid, long handle, metal bottom, marked on the side directly under the handle with: Range Toppers, N-1 ½-B 1 ½ quart Not for microwave use Corning, NY, USA 1180 MA, **$24.50.**

Wild Flower, marked on bottom: RangeToppers™, N-1 ½-B 1 ½ quart Not for microwave use Corning, NY, USA 1180 MA.

Wild Flower, teapot, #P-104, 5.5" tall, 6" wide, 6 cup, marked on side: Corning Ware® P-104 6 cup Corning, NY, USA, 11180MA, **$9.50**.

Wild Flower.
Back: cutting board, 14" long, 10" wide, 5 plastic tab feet on bottom, no mark, **$9.50**. **Top right:** sauce pan, covered, #P-81-B, 1 pint, 2" tall, 6" wide, glass lid, marked on bottom: Corning Ware® P-81-B 1 pint, Range – oven-microwave Corning, NY. USA 179 MA; marked on lid: Pyrex® P 81 C, **$7.50; left:** casserole, covered, #A-2-B, 1.75 quart, 2" tall, 8.5" tall, glass lid, marked on handles: A-2-B 2 liter and Corning Ware®, **$9.50**.

French White

A new style of the All White was offered in 1977 and was called French White. All of these pieces had an exterior finish of pleats. The pieces were designed for the fashion conscious consumer of today that set an elaborate table. The pieces offered were baking items without handles that would look chic on the table. French White was discontinued in 1985.

French White. **Top:** 115 ml, 1.75" tall, 3.5" wide, marked on the bottom – Corning Ware® Made in USA 4 oz. 115 ml, **$5.00; bottom:** #F-15-B, 1.5" tall, 4.75" wide, 7.25" long, 16 ounce, marked on the bottom – Corning Ware® F-15-B 16 ounce for oven and microwave Corning, NY USA 11181 MA, **$5.00**.

French White, #F-16-B, 2.25" tall, 5.5" wide, 500ml, round, plastic lid with blue tab, **$6.50 each. Left:** shown up right to show lid; **right:** shown flat to show shape.

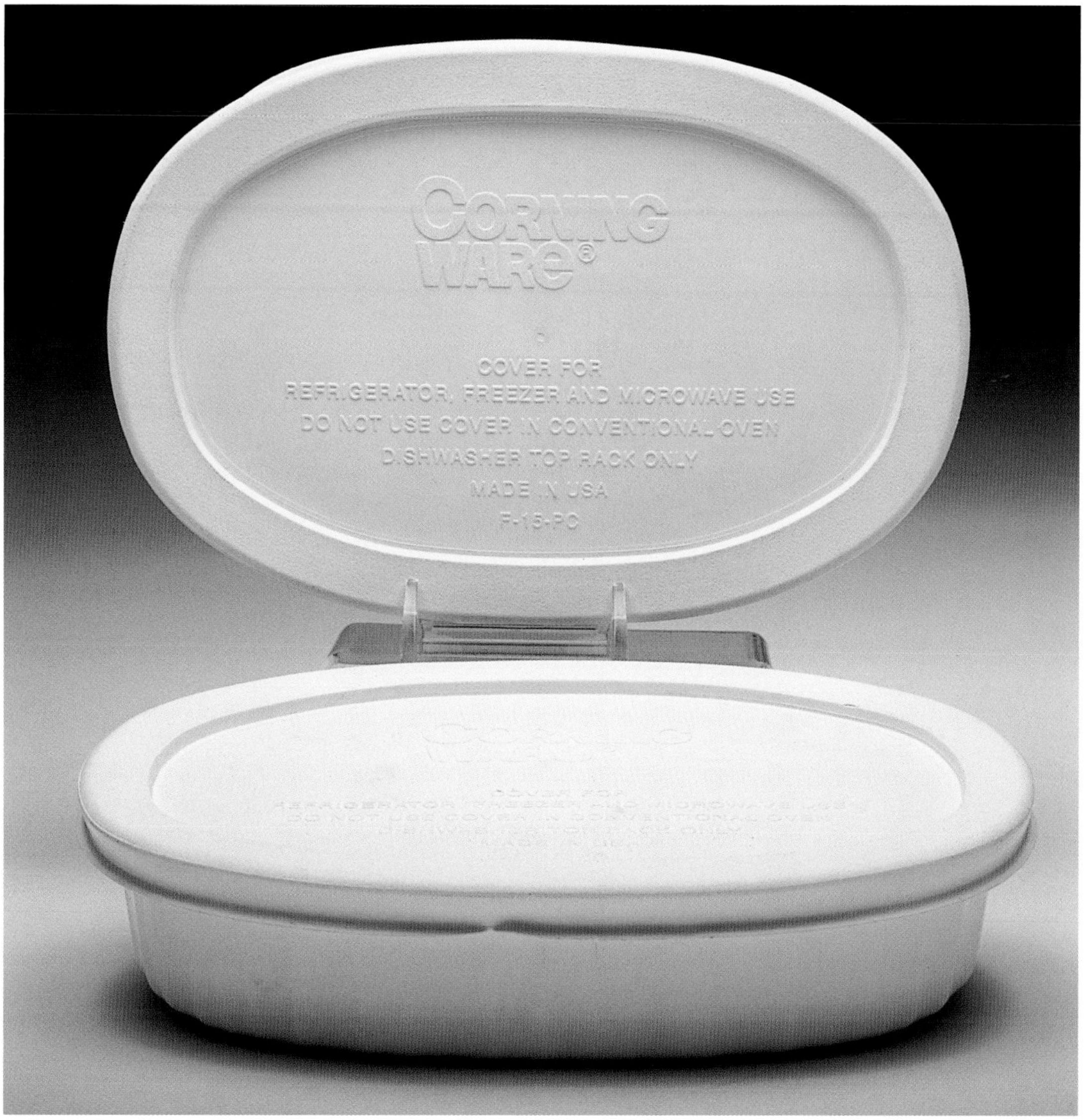

French White, storage container, #F-15-B, 1.75" tall, 7.5" long, 5" wide, 1 pint, plastic lid, marked on the bottom: Corning Ware® F-15-B 475 ML 12, **$6.50 each.** **Back:** upright view to show marking on plastic lid; **front:** flat view to show shape.

French White, Quiche pan, #F-8-B, 8.75" wide, round, marked on the bottom with: Corning Ware® F-8-B 20cm, **$5.00.**

French White, storage container, #F-23-B, 1.75" tall, 6" wide, 9.5" long, 700ml, plastic lid with blue pull tab, marked on the bottom: Corning Ware® F-23-B 700 ML Made in USA 23, **$8.50**.

French White, casserole, covered, #F-6-B, 2" tall, 8.5" wide, 11" long, 1.8 liter, glass lid, marked on the bottom: Corning Ware® F-6-B 1.8 liter, **$9.50**.

French White, casserole, covered, #F-1 ½-B, 4.75" tall, 9.5" long, 7.5" wide, 1 ½ quart, oblong, glass lid, marked on the bottom: Corning Ware® Microwave and Oven Safe 1 ½ QT 1.4 L French White, **$9.50**.

French White, casserole, covered, #F-5-B, 3" tall, 7.75" wide, 1.6 liter, round, glass lid, marked on bottom: Corning Ware® F-5-B 1.6 liter, **$9.50**.

French White with blue trim, casserole, covered, #F-24-B, 2.25" tall, 6.5" wide, 725ml, plastic lid, marked on the bottom: Corning Ware® F-24-B 725ml Made in USA, **$8.50**.

French White with gold, soufflé dish, #F-5-B, 3" tall, 7.75" wide, 1.6 liter, **$7.50**.

French White with gold, oval baker, #F-12-B, 2.5" tall, 7.25" wide, 9.5" long, 1.8 liter, marked on the bottom: Corning Ware® F-12-B 1.8 liter Made in USA 10, **$8.50**.

Strawberry Sunday

Detail of Strawberry Sunday.

Strawberry Sunday was introduced in 1983 as a catalog exclusive. It was not offered in any retail stores. The eight-piece set consisted of a covered 2.5 quart, a covered 1.5 quart and two each of the covered petite pans. A matching teapot could also be ordered as part of this exclusive offering. This was also the first new pattern to have its pieces called covered casseroles.

Strawberry Sunday, petite pan, #P-43-B, 2.25" tall, 5.25" wide, 2.5 cups, plastic lid, marked on the bottom: Corning Ware® P-43-B 700mL, **$7.50.**

Jardin

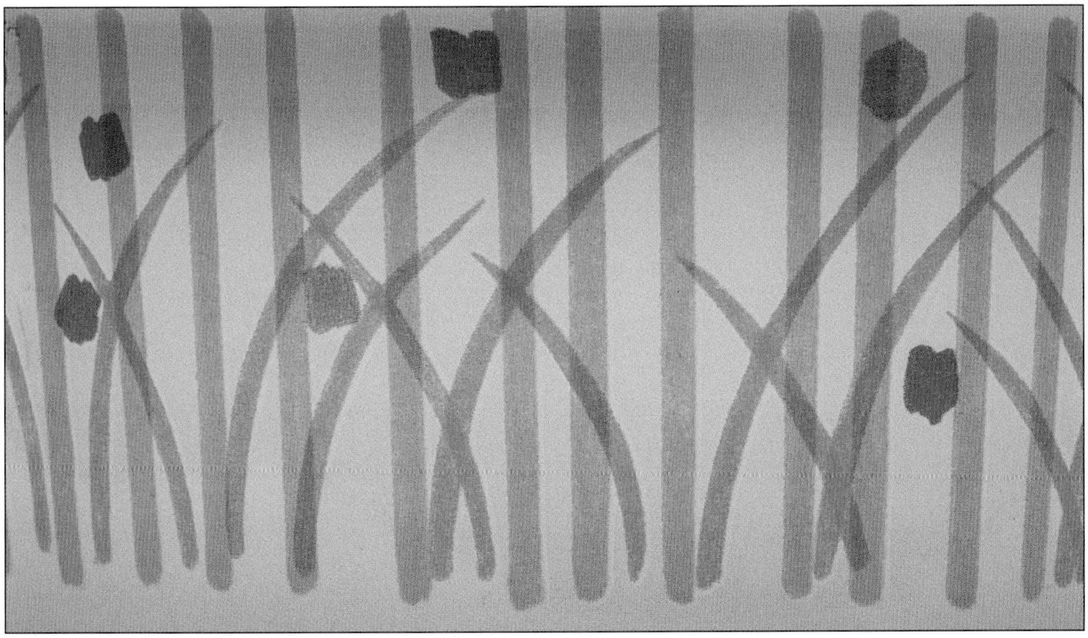

Detail of Jardin pattern.

Jardin was part of the Classic Elegance line. At first the pattern looks like it was set against French White, but the background is actually gray lines. The dainty petite flowers create a simple design. The pattern was made in the mid 1980s.

Jardin, casserole, covered, #C-125-B, 3.5" tall, 10.5" wide, 2.5 liter, round, glass lid, marked on the bottom: freezer to oven C-125-B 2.5 liter Classic Elegance by Corning microwave safe, **$14.50**.

Deco

Deco is an accurate description of this pattern. The simplistic black lines set against the stark white background create a unique pattern. This pattern had a limited production and was only offered in 1985.

Deco, roaster, open, #3306, 2" tall, 12.5" long, 2 quart, **$12.00.** *Photo courtesy of Replacements, Ltd.*

Pastel Bouquet

Detail of Pastel Bouquet pattern.

Pastel Bouquet was introduced in 1985 and featured a soft pastel bunch of wildflowers. This pattern was designed to appeal to a younger person with its softer colors. The pattern covered the pan and went completely around it. From here on out, most of the new patterns would be offered in a Trio Set Special. Pastel bouquet was discontinued in 1990.

Pastel Bouquet, open roaster, #A-21-B, 2.5" tall, 11.5" wide, 14.5" long, marked under the rim: Corning Ware® A-21 12 ¼ x 10 ½ x 2 ¼ inch range – oven – microwave Corning, NY USA 1189 MA, **$13.50.**

Pastel Bouquet, petite pan, #P-43-B, 2.25" tall, 5.25" wide, 2.5 cups, plastic lid, marked on the bottom with: Corning Ware® P-43-B 700ml, **$7.50.**

Pastel Bouquet. **Left:** #A-1 ½ -B, 2.75" tall, 7" wide, 1.5 liter, glass lid, marked on the handles: on one side – Corning Ware®, on the other side – A-1 ½ -B 1.5 liter, **$8.50; right:** #P-43-B, 2.25" tall, 5.25" wide, 2.5 cups, glass lid, marked on the bottom with: Corning Ware® P-43-B 700ml, **$9.50.**

Pastel Bouquet, casserole, covered, #A-2-B, 4.5" tall, 8.5" wide, 2 liter, glass lid, marked on underside of handles: Corning Ware® 5 A-2-B 2 liter, **$9.50**.

Pastel Bouquet, casserole, covered, #A-10-B, 2" tall, 10.25" wide, 2.5 liter, glass lid, marked on underside of handles: Corning Ware® A-10-B 2.5 liter, **$12.50**.

Pastel Bouquet, casserole, covered, #A-5-B, 4.25" tall, 10.25" wide, 5 liter, glass lid, marked on handles: 4 06 A-5-B 5 liter Corning Ware®, **$22.50**.

Pastel Bouquet, Casseroles, covered, glass lid.
Left: #A-2-B, 4.75" tall, 8.5" wide, 2 liter, marked on handles: A-2-B 2 liter and Corning Ware®, **$9.50; Right:** #A-1-B, 3.75" tall, 7" wide, 1 liter, no mark on bottom, marked on handles: A-1-B 1 liter and Corning Ware®, **$7.50.**

Pastel Bouquet, covered casseroles, glass lid. **Left:** #A-3-B, 3.75" tall, 8.5" wide, 3 liter, marked under the handle: 5A-3-B 3 liter Corning Ware®, **$11.50; right:** #A-1 ½-B, 2.75" tall, 7" wide, 1.5 liter, marked under the handle – A-1 ½-B 1.5 liter Corning Ware®, **$8.50**.

Shadow Iris

Detail of Shadow Iris pattern.

The beautiful flag iris provided the theme for the new Shadow Iris pattern in 1986. The stately purple flower set against the green stalk provided a subtle accent that encouraged new homemakers to set up this pattern in their kitchens. There were five covered casseroles, petite pans, teapot and an open roaster. A coordinating Shadow Iris pattern was also made in Corelle®. This pattern would run about ten years before it was ended in 1995.

Shadow Iris, petite pan, #P-43-B, 3" tall, 5.75" wide, 22 ounces, plastic lid, marked on bottom: Corning Ware® P-43-B 700ML, **$7.50.**

Shadow Iris.
Left: casserole, covered, #A-1-B, 2″ tall, 7″ wide, 1 liter, glass lid, marked on handle, Corning Ware®, **$7.50**. **Right:** casserole, covered, #A-1.5-B, 2.75″ tall, 7″ wide, 1.5 liter, glass lid, marked on handle: Corning Ware®, **$8.50.**

Shadow Iris, casserole, covered, #A-1.5-B, 4.75″ tall, 7″ wide, 1.5 liter, glass lid, marked on handle, sets on metal cradle, bottom of metal cradle is marked: bottom P-11-M-1 Corning Ware®, **$9.50.**

Shadow Iris, casserole, covered, #A-2-B, 2.5″ tall, 8.5″ wide, 2 liter, glass lid, marked on handles: A-2-B 2 liter Corning Ware®, **$9.50.**

Shadow Iris, casserole, covered, #A-3-B, 3.75" tall, 8.5" wide, 3 liter, glass lid, marked on the underside of the handles: Corning Ware® 6 07 A-3-B 3 liter, **$14.50.**

Shadow Iris, fry pan, #S-10-B, 1.75" tall, 10.75" wide, waffle like texture on bottom of inside, marked on the handle: Corning Ware® S-10-B 10IN, **$17.50**.

Shadow Iris. **Top**: #A-3-B, 3.75" tall, 8.5" wide, 3 liter, glass lid; **bottom**: Rival Crock-Pot, 6.25" tall, 8.75" wide, square, marked on front: Rival Crock Pot with Corning Ware®, **$24.50 set.** **Note:** The crock pot is hard to find in good working condition.

Shadow Iris, casserole, covered, #A-10-B, 2.25" tall, 10.25" wide, 2.5 liter, glass lid, marked on handles: A-10-B 2.5 liter Corning Ware® 4 14, **$12.50.**

Shadow Iris, casserole, covered, glass lid. **Top right:** #A-3-B, 3.75" tall, 8.5" wide, 3 liter, marked on the underside of the handles: on one side – Corning Ware®, on the other – A-3-B, **$14.50; bottom Left:** #A-5-B, 4.25" tall, 10.25" wide, 5 liter, marked on the underside of the handles: on one side – Corning Ware®, on the other – A-5-B 5 liter, **$22.50.**

Shadow Iris, saucepan, covered, #S-81-B, 2" tall, 5.75" wide, .5 liter, glass lid, marked on handle: Corning Ware® S-81-B 0.5L, **$7.50.**

Shadow Iris, Corelle® dinnerware. **Left:** plate, 7" wide, marked on the back: Corelle® by Corning microwavable no broiler or stovetop Made in USA, **$2.00; right:** plate, 10" wide, marked on the back: Corelle® by Corning, Corning NY USA, microwave safe, not for broiler or stovetop use, **$4.00; front:** mug, 3.5" tall, 3.25" wide, 8 ounces, **$3.00.**

Shadow Iris, tea kettle, go along item, 6" tall to top of lid, 9" wide from tip of spout to side, metal, marked on the bottom: Lincoware® Made in Taiwan, **$12.50.**

Peach Floral

Detail of Peach Floral Pattern

Peach Floral was introduced in 1987 and featured a peachy orange cluster of flowers. In this pattern were five covered casseroles, petite pans, and an open roaster. This was another of the softer pastel patterns that appealed to a younger generation. After a short four year run, the pattern was retired in 1991.

Peach Floral, casserole, covered, #A 1 ½ B, 2.75" tall, 7" wide, 1.5 liter, glass lid, marked on the handles: on one side – Corning Ware®, on the other – A-1 ½ -B 1.5 liter, **$8.50.**

Peach Floral, casserole, covered, #A-2-B, 2.5″ tall, 8.5″ wide, 2 liter, glass lid, marked on the handles: on one side – Corning Ware®, on the other – A-2-B 2 liter, **$9.50**.

Peach Floral, casserole, covered, glass lids. **Left:** #A-10-B, 2″ tall, 10.25″ wide, 2.5 liter, marked on the handles: on one side – Corning Ware®, on the other – A-10-B 2.5 liter, **$12.50; right:** #A-1-B, 2″ tall, 7″ wide, 1 liter, marked on the handles: on one side – Corning Ware®, on the other – A-1-B 1 liter, **$7.50**.

Peach Floral, casserole, covered, A-3-B, 3.85″ tall, 8.5″ wide, 3 liter, glass lid, marked on the underside of the handles: on one side, Corning Ware®, on other one, 17 A-3-B 3 liter, **$14.50**.

Country Cornflower

Detail of Country Cornflower pattern.

In 1988 the Blue Cornflower pattern was discontinued. A year later the pattern received an updated look and given the new name of Country Cornflower. The Cornflower was given a softer blue look and set in a basket with a bow. A few pinkish flowers added to the touch to give the pattern a country look. Country Cornflower had five covered casseroles, an open roaster and a petite pan. It was also offered as a Trio set and a Chef Master set. The pattern was discontinued in 1993.

Country Cornflower, casserole, covered, A-1-B, 1.85" tall, 7" wide, 1 liter, glass lid, marked on underside of handles: Corning Ware® A-1-B 1 liter, **$8.50.**

Country Cornflower, decanter, 10" tall, 4.75" wide, 2 quart, crystal with blue silk screen, marked along the bottom edge: 2 QT 2 L Pyrex® Made in USA Caution for cold liquids only Do not use metal stirrer Not for freezer or range top 7520, **$9.50. Note:** Pyrex go along item.

Country Cornflower, casserole, covered, #A-3-B, 3.75" tall, 8.5" wide, 3 liter, glass lid, marked on underside of handles: Corning Ware® 8 02 A-3-B 3 liter, **$14.50**.

Country Cornflower, petite pan, covered, #P-43-B , 2.35" tall, 5.25" wide, 700ml, plastic lid, marked on bottom: Corning Ware® P-43-B 700ml, **$7.50**.

Country Cornflower, kitchen labels, 3" long, 2" wide, self sticking, count of 24, package says: Corning Coordinates Perfect for canning or freezing plus hundreds of other uses, **$1.00. Note:** Go along item, not made by Corning. When both of our daughters were in 4-H they used these labels on their food preservations they entered at fair.

Peony

Detail of Peony pattern.

For those that love the Peony flower in their garden, this would make a wonderful addition to a kitchen. It was only offered for one year in 1989. There were several sizes of saucepans and a couple of skillets offered in this pattern.

Peony, sauce pan, covered, #P-81-B, 2″ tall, 6″ wide, 1 pint, glass lid, marked, **$7.50.** *Photo courtesy of Replacements, Ltd.*

Peony, casserole, covered, #A-2-B, 2.5″ tall, 8.5″ wide, 2 liter, glass lid, marked, **$9.50.** *Photo courtesy of Replacements, Ltd.*

Classic Black

In 1990, the normally white Pyroceram® was given some color. Classic Black came from the French White pattern that was turned black. This was a real departure for Corning and created a stunning appearance at the table. The striking black color appealed to a new consumer and allowed a new elegance at a meal. The Classic Black was only offered until 1995.

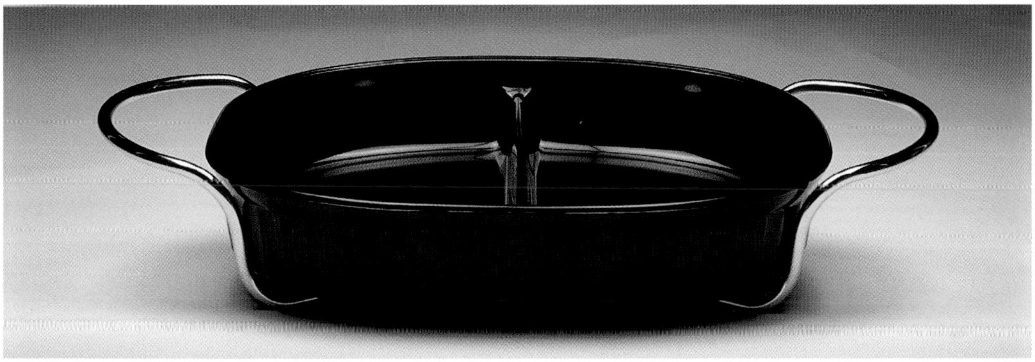

Classic Black, #F-6-B/ MC-6-B, 2″ tall, 8.25″ wide, 10.75″ long, 1.8 liter, 2 part, chrome tray, marked on the bottom: Corning Ware® F-6-B 1.8 liter MC-6-B 1.8 liter, **$14.50.**

Forever Yours

Detail of Forever Yours pattern (heart design).

Another departure from the white Pyroceram®, came with the introduction of the beige color in 1990 on two different patterns. This new color was the first major change in the cookware line since 1958, when it was introduced. Market research showed that the consumer wanted some cookware in a color other than white. Forever Yours featured a pink heart motif. It was described as having an Americana feel with a calico country look. This beige pattern was marketed with amber lids instead of the regular crystal. Consumers could also use crystal lids since they were all the same size. In this pattern there were five covered casseroles, an open roaster and a petite pan. It was also offered as a Trio set and a Chef Master set. There was a matching Forever Yours in Corelle® to compliment this pattern. Forever Yours was discontinued in 1994.

Forever Yours covered casseroles, glass lids . **Left:** #A-1 ½-B, 3" tall, 7" wide, dark lid, 1.5 liter, marked on handles: Corning Ware®, A-1 ½-B, **$9.50; right:** #A-1 ½-B, 3" tall, 7" wide, 1.5 liter, clear lid, marked on handles: Corning Ware®, A-1 ½-B, **$8.50**.

Forever Yours, casseroles, dark glass lids. **Left:** #A-2-B, 2.5" tall, 8.25" wide, 2 liter, marked on the underside of the handles: on one side – Corning Ware® and on the other- A-2-B 2 liter, **$9.50; right:** #A-1-B, 2" tall, 6.75" wide, 1 liter, marked on the underside of the handles: on one side – Corning Ware® and on the other – A-1-B 1 liter, **$7.50.**

Forever Yours, 0pen roaster, #A-21-B-N, 2.5" tall, 11" wide, 12.5" long, marked on the underside of the handles: on one handle – Corning Ware® and on the other – A-21-B-N 12 ¼ x 10 ½ x 2 ½, **$12.50.**

Forever Yours, Corelle® dinnerware. **Back:** platter, 10" wide, 12.25" long, marked on the back: Corelle® by Corning microwavable no broiler or stovetop Made in USA, **$9.50; center left:** plate, 6.75" wide, marked on the back: Corelle® by Corning microwavable no broiler or stovetop Made in USA, **$2.00; center right:** plate, 10.25" wide, marked on the back: Corelle® by Corning microwavable no broiler or stovetop Made in USA, **$4.00; front:** mug, 3.75" tall, 3" wide, 6 ounces, marked on the bottom: Corning USA microwave ok, **$3.00.**

Symphony

Detail of Symphony pattern.

Symphony was the other pattern introduced in 1990 in a beige color. This pattern featured a bouquet of different types of flowers. In the catalog this pattern was described as "old world charm." Like Forever Yours, this pattern also was marketed with amber lids, though crystal lids could also be used. Forever Yours had five covered casseroles, an open roaster and a petite pan. It was also offered as a Trio set and a Chef Master set. This pattern was also discontinued in 1994.

Symphony, casserole, covered, #A-1-B, 2" tall, 7" wide, 1 liter, dark glass lid, marked on handles: Corning Ware® A-1-B 1 liter, **$7.50.**

Symphony, casserole, covered, #A-2-B, 2.5″ tall, 8.5″ wide, 2 liter, dark glass lid, marked on the handles: on one side – Corning Ware®, on the other side – A-2-B 2 liter, **$9.50.**

Symphony, casserole, covered, #A-5-B, 4″ tall, 10.25″ wide, 5 liter, glass lid, metal cradle, marked on the underside of the handles: on one side – Corning Ware®, on the other – A-5-B 5 liter, **$24.50.**

Silk and Roses

Detail of Silk and Roses pattern.

Silk and Roses was first offered in 1991 and resembled a tapestry from the Victorian period. The red roses were set against a textured blue ribbon to create a unique design. The appearance of this pattern was made to appeal to the modern consumer that was attracted to antique settings. Silk and Roses first appeared as a Corelle® dinnerware pattern before it was made as cookware. In this pattern were five covered casseroles, an open roaster and a petite pan. Also to coordinate with it were grab it bowls in beige. A Trio and Chef Master sets were available in this pattern. In 1994, this pattern was retired.

Silk and Roses, Casserole grouping, covered, glass lids, marked on the underside of one handle: Corning Ware. **Back:** #A-2-B, 2.5" tall, 8.5" wide, 2 liter, marked on the underside of other handle: A-2-B 2 liter, **$11.50; front left:** #A-1 1/2-B, 3" tall, 7" wide, 1.5 liter, marked on the underside of other handle: #A-1 1/2-B 1.5 liter, **$9.50; front right:** #A-10-B, 2.25" tall, 10.25" wide, 2.5 liter, marked on the underside of other handle: A-10-B 2.5 liter, **$12.50.**

Silk and Roses, open roaster, #A-21-B-N, 2.5" tall, 10.75" wide, 12.75" long, marked on the handles: on one side – Corning Ware® 89A and on the other side – A-21-B-N 12 ¼ x 10 ½ x 2 ½, **$14.50.**

Silk and Roses, cutting board, 15" long, 12" wide, Crystal, **$9.50.** **Note:** This is a Pyrex item.

Abundance

Detail of Abundance pattern.

Abundance was another pattern to appear on the beige color of Pyroceram®. Abundance was first offered in 1992 and was only continued for four years when it ended in 1996. This was the first Corning pattern to feature a fruit bouquet in its design. Abundance was made in five covered casseroles, an open roaster and a petite pan. Abundance was also made as a Corelle® pattern. This pattern was also coordinated with amber lids.

Abundance, casserole, covered, #A-2-B-21, 2.5" tall, 8.5" wide, 2 quart, glass lid, marked on handles: Corning Ware® A-2-B-21 2L USA, **$9.50**.

Abundance, Corelle® platter, 10" wide, 12.25" long, marked on the back: Corelle® by Corning microwavable no broiler or stovetop Made in USA, **$9.50.**

Orchard Rose

Detail of Orchard Rose pattern.

Orchard Rose was part of the Corning cookware line for only one year in 1992. The floral design was meant to imitate an English country garden. This beautiful arrangement appealed to many types of consumers who loved the look of their gardens. With this pattern, the garden could become part of the kitchen. There were four covered casseroles and an open roaster made in this pattern. A Chef set could also be purchased.

Orchard Rose, #A-1-B, 2" tall, 7" wide, 1 liter, glass lid, marked on the under side of the handles: on one side – Corning Ware®, on the other – A-1-B 1 liter, **$7.50.**

French White Delicious

Detail of French White Delicious pattern.

French White Delicious featured the gorgeous red apple set against the French White pattern. This was the first time that Corning had put a decoration on their French White. The apple had always been a popular design for other companies and now this was the first time Corning had emphasized this favorite fruit. This pattern had a country charm about it. There were only two sizes of covered casseroles made, a 2.5 quart round and 2.5 quart oval. A matching Corelle® pattern was also made. French White Delicious was only offered for one year in 1992.

Sun Garden

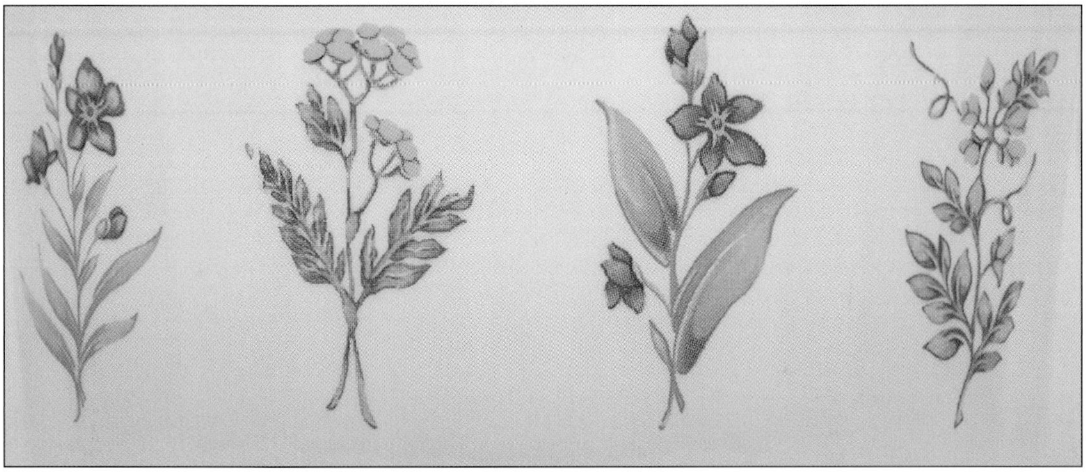

Detail of Sun Garden pattern.

This pattern featured four different flowers set against the French White background. We did not find a date for this pattern but since Delicious was the first pattern used with the French White, the Sun Garden had to follow in a previous year.

Sun Garden, #F-5-B, 3" tall, 7.75" wide, 1.6 liter, round, marked on the bottom: Corning Ware® F-5-B 1.6 Liter 20 Made in USA, **$9.50**.

Blue Dusk

Detail of Blue Dusk pattern.

Blue Dusk became a new cookware pattern in 1994. The small fanciful purple flowers were accented with green stems to create this pattern. This was another attempt by Corning to attract the gardener to have a cookware pattern that brought the outdoors into their kitchens. In this pattern were six covered casseroles and an open roaster. Blue Dusk was discontinued in 1997.

Blue Dusk, casserole, covered, #A-1 ½-B, 2.75" tall, 7" wide, 1.5 liter, glass lid, marked on the handles: on one side – Corning Ware® and on the other – A-1 ½ -B 1.5 liter, **$9.50**.

Blue Dusk, #A-2-B-21, 2.5" tall, 8.5" wide, 2 liter, glass lid, marked on handles: Corning Ware® A-2-B-21 2L USA, **$9.50.**

Blue Dusk, roaster, open, #A-21-B-N, 2.5" tall, 10.5" wide, 12.25" long, 4 quart, marked on handle Corning Ware®, **$13.50.**

Garden Harvest

Detail of Garden Harvest pattern.

Another new pattern for 1994 was the Garden Harvest. This was another attempt by Corning to feature a pattern with colorful vegetables from the garden. The bright red tomatoes were accented with yellow corn and green peas. It must have been a delight for all gardeners to have in their kitchen. Garden Harvest had five covered casseroles and an open roaster. This pattern was discontinued two years later in 1996.

Quilt

The Corning Life Styles collection in 1994 emphasized the American spirit with two country quilt designs. One pattern was simply called Quilt. It featured a green box set inside a red star on larger pieces and just a heart on smaller items. The patchwork design gave that feel of home with a country touch to it. A coordinating Corelle® dinnerware was also made. There were only three covered casseroles in this pattern, but, besides a matching Corelle® dinnerware, there also were coordinating glassware, linens and accessories. The pattern was only offered for one year.

Another version of this pattern was called Blue Star. The blue eight pointed star alternated with a smaller diamond for this design. Depending on the size of the piece there could be one to three stars on them.

Quilt, #A-2-B-21, 2.5" tall, 8.5" wide, 2 liter, glass lid, marked on handles: Corning Ware® A-2-B-21 2L USA, **$12.50.** *Photo courtesy of Replacements, Ltd.*

Blue Heart

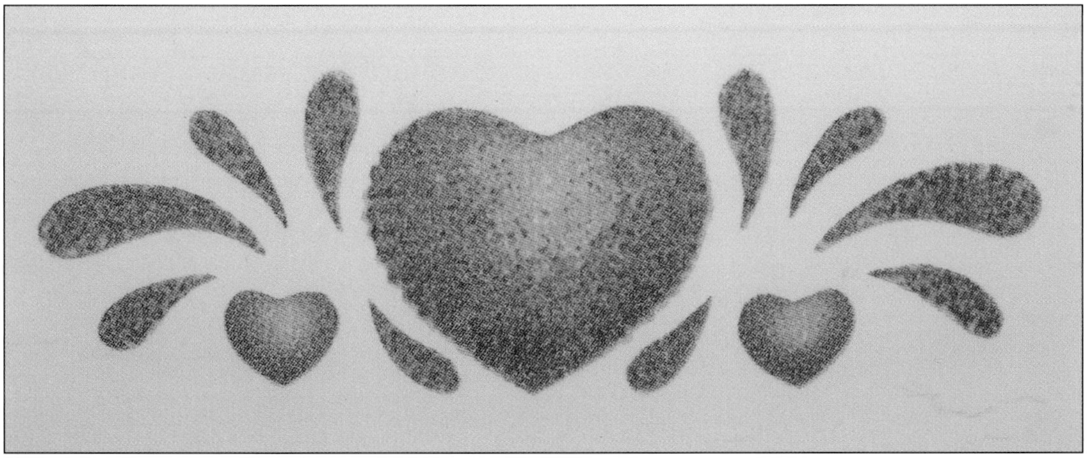

Detail of Blue Heart pattern.

Blue Heart was an extension of the Quilt pattern, which had red hearts. The design featured a blue heart with a sponge effect. While the cookware only featured three covered casseroles, there was an extensive Corelle® line along many different types of accessories.

Blue Heart, casserole, covered, #A-2-B, 2.5" tall, 8.5" wide, 2 liter, glass lid, marked on the underside of handles: on one side-Corning Ware® Made in USA and on the other side – A-2-B 2L USA 14. **$9.50**

Casual Elegance

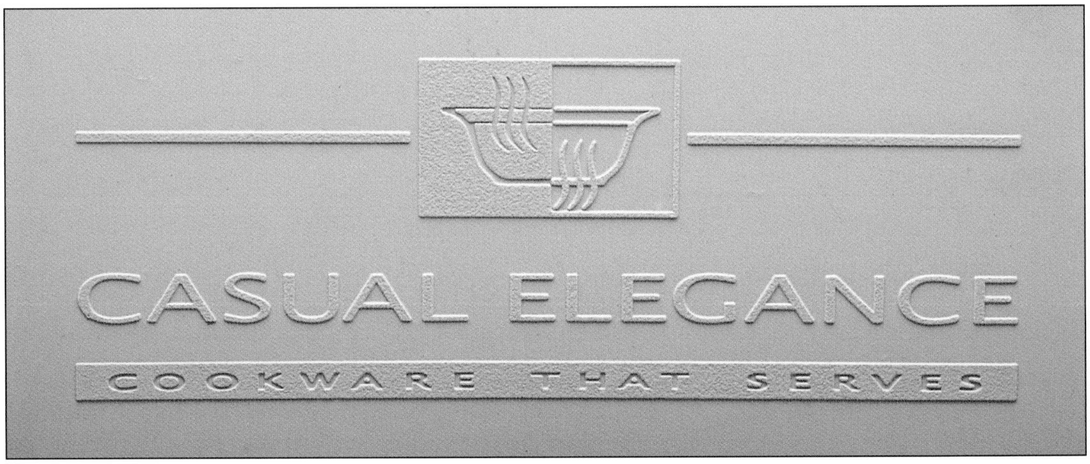

Detail of Casual Elegance mark.

Casual Elegance was a white floral first offered in 1995 and continued until 1998. The pattern was designed to appeal to a sophisticated cook. There was a simple flower set on a new sleek style. It was also referred to as White Flora in the catalog. The glass lids for this pattern were also of a new style and featured an open handle for picking up.

Casual Elegance, casserole, covered, #L-22, 3" tall, 11.75" wide, round, glass lid, marked on bottom: L-22 11 Corning Oven Broiler Microwave Freezer, **$12.50**.

Casual Elegance, casserole, covered, #L-32, 2.25″ tall, 10″ wide, 14″ long, oval, embossed floral on rim, glass lid, marked on bottom: L-32 10 Corning Oven Broiler Microwave Freezer, **$12.50.**

Casual Elcgance, casserole, covered, #L-15, 2.5″ tall, 11.75″ wide, 15″ long, plastic lid, marked on the bottom: L-15 07 Corning Oven Broiler Microwave Freezer, **$12.50.**

English Meadow

Detail of English Meadow on French White pattern.

English Meadow was only offered in 1995. The petite flowers were set against the French White pattern. The little flowers resemble scallop-shaped butter cookies. The three colors of blue, red and yellow flowers are on trailing branches of green leaves. In this pattern were two sizes of round covered casseroles along with an oval covered casserole.

English Meadow, casserole, covered, #F-2-B, 2.5" tall, 8.5" wide, 11" long, 2.5 liter, marked on the bottom: Corning Ware® F-2-B 2.5 liter, **$9.50.**

Callaway

Detail of Calloway (Ivy) pattern.

Callaway was another new pattern in 1995 that set green ivy against the white background. The clusters of the beautiful green ivy leaves were very attractive. The pattern featured two sizes of round covered casseroles along with an oval covered casserole. Callaway remained in production until 1998.

Calloway (Ivy), casserole, covered, #A-2-B, 2" tall, 8.5"wide, 2 liter, glass lid, marked on the underside of the handles: Corning Ware® Made in USA A-2-B 2L USA, **$9.50**.

Lyrics

Detail of Lyrics pattern (tulips).

Lyrics was introduced in 1995. The black tulip flowers set against the white background created a stark contrast that was very appealing. This is a classic Art Deco style of decoration that would appeal to many people. There were four covered casseroles along with an open roaster made in this pattern. A beginning set could be purchased as a Trio set. The Lyrics pattern was only offered until 1996.

Lyrics, casserole, covered, #A-1 ½-B, 2.75" tall, 7" wide, 1.5 liter, glass lid, marked on the handles: on one side – Corning Ware® and on the other – A-1 ½ -B 1.5 liter, **$12.50.** *Photo courtesy of Replacements, Ltd.*

Lyrics, casserole, covered, #A-2-B, 2" tall, 8.5"wide, 2 liter, glass lid, marked on the underside of the handles: Corning Ware® Made in USA A-2-B 2L USA 14, **$12.50.** *Photo courtesy of Replacements, Ltd.*

Lyrics, roaster, open, #A-21-B-N, 2.5" tall, 11" wide, 12.5" long, marked on the underside of the handles: on one handle – Corning Ware® and on the other – A-21-B-N 12 1/4x10 1/2x2 ½, **$16.50.**

Rosemarie

Detail of Rosemarie pattern

Rosemarie features petite pink flowers set with green leaves. The pattern was offered from 1995 to 1997. This was another decoration set on the beige cookware. The style of the flower kind of reminds one of the lily of the valley. For this pattern there were four covered casseroles along with an open roaster. A Trio set could be purchased as a nice wedding gift.

Rosemarie, Casserole, covered, #A-1 1/2-B, 2.75" tall, 7"wide, 1.5 liter, glass lid, marked on the underside of the handles: Corning Ware® Made in USA A-1 1/2-B 1.5 Liter 17, **$9.50**

Rosemarie, covered, #A-2-B, 2" tall, 8.5"wide, 2 liter, glass lid, marked on the underside of the handles: Corning Ware® Made in USA A-2-B 2L USA 14, **$9.50.** *Photo courtesy of Replacements, Ltd.*

English Breakfast

English Breakfast was another attempt by Corning to offer a beige cookware. Introduced in 1995, it was only produced until 1996. This pattern featured a cluster of flowers inside an irregular outline consisting of two colors. This was another pattern developed from an English theme. In the English Breakfast pattern, there were four covered casseroles along with an open roaster made in this pattern. A beginning set could be purchased as a Trio set.

English Breakfast, 5.75" tall, 10.25" wide, 3 liter, glass lid, marked, **$14.50.**

Sunsations

Sunsations was actually a play on words to describe this new cookware pattern in 1996. The beautiful yellow sunflower was the theme of this pattern creating a sensational effect. There were four covered casseroles offered along with an open roaster. A gorgeous Corelle® pattern coordinated with this cookware. Sunsations was only offered until 1997.

Sunsations, casserole, covered, # A-2-B, 2.5" tall, 8.5" wide, 2 quart, glass lid, marked on handle: A-2-B 2L USA, **$9.50.**

Sunsations, casseroles, covered, glass lid. **Top:** #A-1 ½ -B, 2.75" tall, 7" wide, 1.5 liter, marked on the handles: on one side -Corning Ware® and on the other – A-1 ½ -B 1.5 liter, **$9.50; bottom:** #A-2-B, 2.5" tall, 8.5" wide, 2 liter, glass lid, marked on underside of handles: Corning Ware® 8 02 A-2-B 2 liter, **$9.50.** *Photo courtesy of Replacements, Ltd.*

Friendship

Detail of Friendship pattern.

Friendship was a soft pastel floral pattern that introduced in 1996. The name of this pattern is frequently used on another one, called Country Festival. Since these patterns are totally different it is not known why this name was used on the other one. There were five covered casseroles along with an open roaster made in this pattern. The Friendship pattern ended in 1997.

Friendship, #A-1 ½ -B, 3" tall, 7" wide, 1.5 liter, glass lid, marked on the under side of the handles: on one side – Corning Ware® Made in USA, on the other side – A-1 ½ -B 1.5 liter, **$8.50.**

Friendship, casserole, covered, #A-2-B, 4.75" tall, 8.25" wide, 2 quart, glass lid, marked on handle: A-2-B 2L USA, **$9.50.**

Summer Blush

Detail of the Summer Blush (Pansy) pattern.

Summer Blush shows off the stunning colors of the wonderful pansy flower. This pattern made its debut in 1996. Five covered casseroles together with an open roaster made up the cookware for this pattern. Summer Blush was also offered as a Corelle® dinnerware pattern. Summer Blush continued until 1998.

Original box showing the Summer Blush trio set.

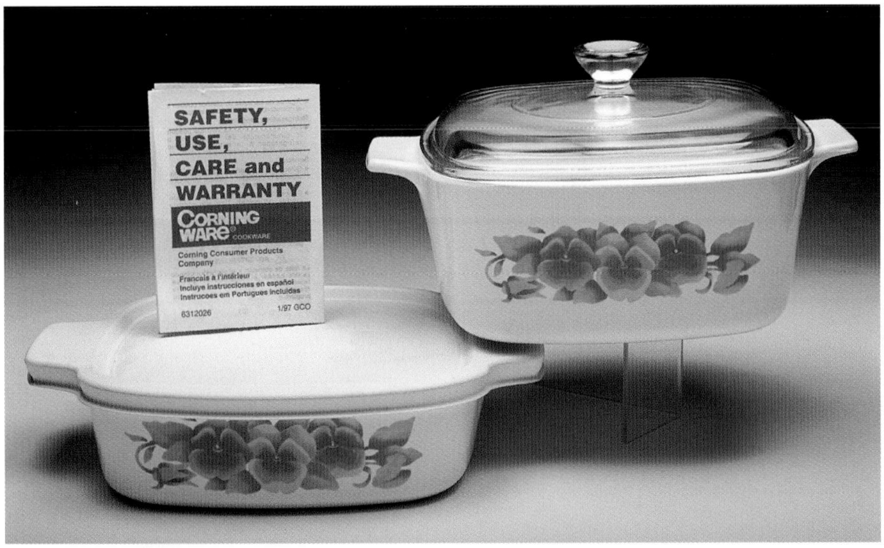

Summer Blush, casseroles, covered. **Back:** original brochure; **left:** #A-1-B, 2″ tall, 7″ wide, 1 liter, plastic lid, marked on the under side of the handles: on one side – Corning Ware® Made in USA and on the other – A-1-B 1 L USA 13, **$8.50; right:** #A-1 ½ -B, 2.85″ tall, 6.75″ wide, 1.5 liter, glass lid, marked on the underside of the handles: on one side – Corning Ware® Made in USA and on the other – A-1 ½-B 1.5 liter 20, **$11.50.**
Note: It is interesting that the box lists the sizes in quarts but they are actually marked in liters.

Summer Blush, casserole, covered, #A-2-B, 2.5″ tall, 8.5″ wide, 2 quart, glass lid, marked on the under side of the handles: on one side – Corning Ware® Made in USA and on the other – A-2-B 2 L USA, **$14.50.**

Summer Blush, Corelle®, dinnerware. **Left:** salad plate, 7.25″ wide, marked on the bottom: Corelle® by Corning microwavable no broiler or stovetop Made in USA **$2.00; right:** dinner plate, 10.25″ wide, marked on the bottom: Corelle® by Corning microwavable no broiler or stovetop Made in USA, **$4.00. Front:** mugs, 3.5″ tall, 8 ounces, shown with front and back views, marked on the bottom: Corning USA Microwave ok, **$3.00.**

Fresh Cut

The beautiful garden tulip provided the theme for the Fresh Cut pattern in 1997. The bright colors of red, orange, green, yellow, and blue provided a rich appeal to this pattern. Coordinating Corelle® dinnerware along with glassware and accessories allowed you to set a magnificent table. There were four covered casseroles and an open roaster. The pattern was discontinued in 1998.

Fresh Cut, casserole, covered, #A-1 ½-B, 19, 2.75″ tall, 7.5″ wide, 1.5 liter, glass lid, **$8.50.**

Blue Velvet

Blue Velvet featured blue roses on this new decoration in 1997. The rose flower is a perennial favorite of many gardeners. A blue pattern set against a white background has also been a favorite among many collectors for years. The combination of the two featured an unbeatable look for a kitchen motif. In this pattern there were four covered casseroles and an open roaster. A coordinating dinnerware pattern in Corelle® could also be purchased. Blue Roses was discontinued in 1998.

Blue Velvet, #A-2-B, 2.5″ tall, 8.5″ wide, 2 quart, glass lid, marked on the under side of the handles: on one side – Corning Ware® Made in USA and on the other – A-2-B 2 L USA, **$11.50.** *Photo courtesy of Replacements, Ltd.*

Fruit Basket

Detail of Fruit Basket pattern showing only the cherry .

Fruit Basket was an accurate description of this pattern since it featured a variety of fruit on the cookware. This pattern debuted in 1997 and ended a year later in 1998. There were five covered casseroles and an open roaster in this pattern. The unique thing of this pattern was putting different fruit on the various sizes of casseroles. The types of fruit used were the apple, cherry and grape. On the two quart size all three fruits were used. The matching Corelle® dinnerware would enable the homemaker to set a beautiful table.

Fruit Basket, casserole, #A-1-B, covered, 2" tall, 7.5" wide, 1 quart, cherry symbol, glass lid, marked on handles: A-1-B 1L USA Corning Ware® Made in USA, **$7.50**.

Detail of Fruit Basket pattern showing all of the fruit.

Fruit Basket, casserole, covered, #A-2-B, 2" tall, 8.5" wide, 2 liter, fruits symbol, glass lid, marked on handles: A-2-B 2L USA 02 Corning Ware®, **$9.50.**

Ocean View

Detail of Ocean View pattern.

Ocean View featured a big departure from the normal Corning theme for their cookware in 1997. The flowing blue ocean waves provided a unique idea for a cookware pattern. The blue set against the white created another striking combination. For this pattern were five covered casseroles and an open roaster. The coordinating Corelle® pattern allowed you to have a special table setting. Ocean View was discontinued in 1998.

Ocean View, casserole, covered, #A-1 ½-B, 2.75" tall, 6.75" wide, 1.5 liter, glass lid, marked on the underside of the handles: on one side, Corning Ware® Made in USA, on other side, A-1 ½-B 1.5 liter 23, **$8.50**.

Ocean View, casserole, covered, #A-1-B, 2" tall, 6.75" wide, 1 liter, marked on the underside of the handles: Corning Ware® Made in USA, on other side, A-1-B 1L USA 11, plastic lid, **$7.50.**

Ocean View, casserole, covered, #A-2-B, 2.5" tall, 8.5" wide, 2 liter, glass lid, marked on the underside of handles: on one side, Corning Ware® Made in USA, on the other side, A-2-B 2L USA 21, **$12.50.**

Group view of Ocean View pattern pieces.

Provincial Blue

Detail of Provincial Blue pattern.

These simple petite blue flowers make s stunning pattern. This pattern was also used as a Corelle® pattern. We couldn't find a date listed for this pattern but it is marked in liters so it was a later pattern from the 1990s.

Provincial Blue, casserole, covered, #A-2-B, 2.5" tall, 8.5" wide, 2 liter, glass lid, marked on the underside of handles: on one side – Corning Ware®, on the other side – A-2-B 2 liter USA, **$9.50.**

My Garden

Detail of My Garden pattern.

There are four different flowers featured along with a butterfly in the garden. This was the first time that we could find that any type of insect was used set against actual flowers. We could not find a date for this pattern but must have been one from the last years since it had the liter measurement on it.

My Garden, casserole, covered, #A-2-B, 2.5" tall, 8.5" wide, 2 liter, glass lid, marked on the handles: on one side – Corning Ware® Made in USA and on the other – A-2-B 2L USA, **$12.50.**

Holiday Tree

Detail of Christmas Tree pattern. **Note**, we could not find the name of this pattern and because of that decided to use the name Christmas Tree until we find the right name.

We do not know the correct name to this pattern. We could not determine whether Holiday Tree or Christmas Tree would be correct since a catalog listing could not be found for this pattern. The green tree with red balls definitely suggests the holiday season. In talking with the librarian we reasoned that this was a limited issue only available for the holiday time and then was discontinued. Without a catalog, we also couldn't provide a date for it. Since we have only found this pattern in the open roaster it is not known what other pieces were made.

Christmas Tree, open roaster, #A-21-B-N, 2.25" tall, 11" wide, 12.5" long, marked on the underside of handles: one side, Corning Ware® and other side, A-21-B-N 12 ¼ x 10 ½ x 2 ½, **$13.50.**

Burgundy/Cobalt-Flower

Detail of Burgundy/Cobalt Flower.

This was another pattern that we could not find a listing for it. The pattern shows off a simple brush stroke of burgundy and cobalt flower petals. The design is set against a white paneled background. Since this is the only piece we have found, it is not known what other pieces were made. Likewise, without a catalog, we can't provide a date for it.

Burgundy/Cobalt flower, saucepan, covered, #1174, 2.5" tall, 6.5" wide, paneled, round with round tab handles, plastic lid, marked on the bottom: Corning 1174, **$8.50.**

Special Orders

While Corning made different patterns through the years for their own catalog, they also made some special pieces for other companies.

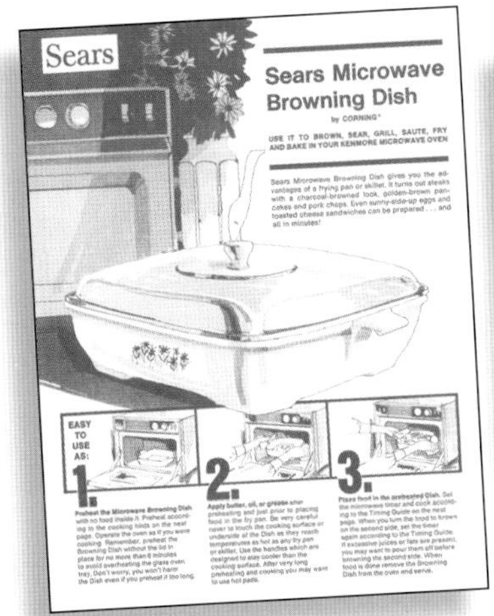

Sears brochure showing browning skillet page 1. *Photo courtesy of Corning Incorporated, Archives.*

Sears brochure showing browning skillet page 2. *Photo courtesy of Corning Incorporated, Archives.*

The #MWA-10 all white browning skillet was developed for the Corning line in the late 1970s specifically for use in the microwave. The four tab feet allowed the browning unit to be raised above the bottom of the microwave. The specially treated bottom enabled the food to brown in the microwave. It was used as a special order item for three different companies. On each of the pans was a different blue symbol on it for the particular company it was made for. There were two different symbols used for Sears: groupings of petite flowers and leaves. The pan was listed in a brochure to be used in the Kenmore microwave oven. A colonial house next to a tree was the design on the pan made for the Amana Radarange. The MW symbol was used on the Montgomery Wards skillet.

Sears, garden of blue flowers, browning skillet, #MW-16, 2.5" tall, 10" wide, 2.5 quart, glass lid, marked on handle: Made for Sears, **$12.50.**

Sears, marked on bottom: Sears Roebuck & Co. microwave browning dish Made for Sears model 8467310 by Corning.

Sears, bouquet of blue flowers, browning skillet, #MW-16, 2.5" tall, 10" wide, 2.5 quart, glass lid, marked on handle: Made for Sears, **$12.50.**

Detail of Sears garden of blue flowers for browning skillet.

Amana, browning skillet, covered, 4″ tall, 7″ wide, glass lid, marked on bottom: Browning skillet Made Expressly for the Amana Radarange Microwave/Oven by Corning Made in USA, **$8.50**.

Pattern detail of Colonial House on Amana.

Amana, browning skillet, #MW-16, 5″ tall, 10.5″ wide, 2.5 quart, glass lid, marked on bottom: browning skillet by Corning, made expressly for Amana Radarange microwave oven, Corning, NY USA 278 MA, **$14.50**.

Inset:
Amana, mark on bottom: Browning skillet Made Expressly for the Amana Radarange Microwave/Oven by Corning Made in USA.

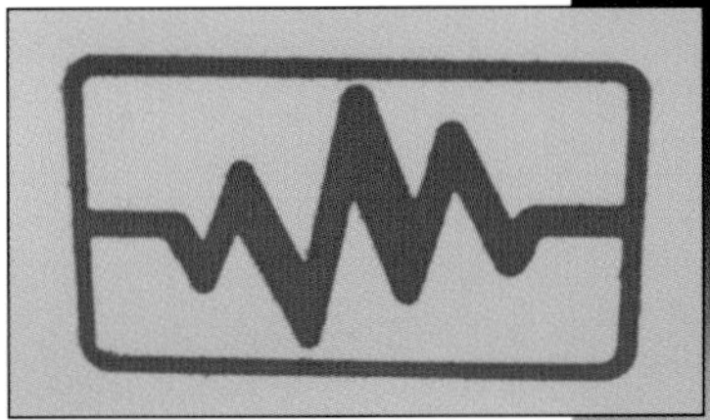

Detail of MW symbol.

MW, browning skillet, 4.25″ tall, 10.5″ wide, 2.5 quart, glass lid, marked on bottom: Electronic Oven browner grille 68-8000 Made expressly for Montgomery Wards Signature by Corning, 1974, **$12.50**.

The Shell Oil Company credit card division offered a special decorated cookware set to their account holders in the early 1970s. A curlicue medallion was offered in Avocado green and the Cornflower blue color. There were two covered saucepans, a petite pan, skillet, loaf pan and the open roaster.

Above, left:
Detail of Blue Medallion pattern.

Above, right:
Detail of Avocado Green Medallion pattern.

Left:
Shell Oil Medallion, open roaster, #P-332, 2.25" tall, 13.5" long, 8.25" wide, 2 quart, marked on bottom: P-332 12x7 1/2x2 Corning Ware® For range and microwave USA, **$12.50.**

Avocado Green Medallion 001. **Left:** casserole, covered, #A-8-B, 2" tall, 8.5" wide, glass lid, marked on the bottom: A-8-B 8x8x1 ¾ Corning Ware® for range and microwave USA, **$9.50; right:** petite pan, #P-41-B, 1.65" tall, 5.25" wide, 1.75 cups, glass lid, marked on the bottom: Corning Ware® P-41-B 1 ¾ cup Made in USA for range & microwave, **$7.50.**

Avocado Green Medallion, petite pan, #P-41-B, 1.65" tall, 5.25" wide, 1.75 cups, plastic lid, marked on the bottom: Corning Ware® P-41-B 1 ¾ cup Made in USA for range & microwave, **$6.50.**

Accessories

In the first years, the side tab handles were small. The cookware was redesigned in 1972 after many suggestions from consumers. The tab handles were made larger to make it easier to pick up. Also, at the same time, the knobs on the glass lids were increased for easier gripping. There were several different sizes of detachable handles used on the cookware.

Comparison of tab handles showing the differences between the narrow and wide styles.

Comparison of the glass lids showing a small and large knob.

Detachable handle for petite pan, #P-41-HG, 5.5" long, metal with black plastic, marked on underside with: Corning Ware®, **$5.00 each. Back:** front view of original box; **front:** top view of the handle.

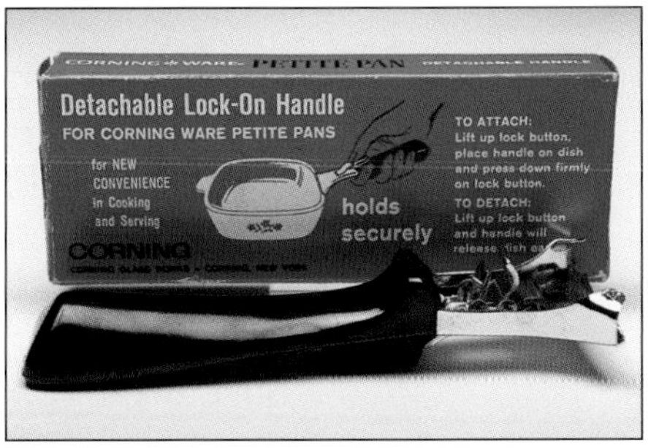

Detachable handle for petite pan, #P-41-HG, 5.5" long, metal with black plastic, marked on underside with: Corning Ware®, **$5.00 each. Back:** back view of box showing directions for use; **front:** underneath view of handle.

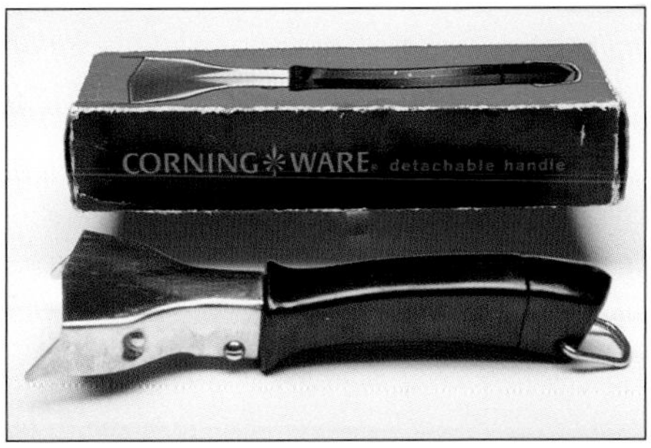

Detachable handle for saucepans, #P-10-HG, 7.5" long, metal with black plastic, end twists for putting on and off, ring on end, marked on the underside with: Corning Ware® Pat. No. 2,851,299, **$5.00 each. Back:** front view of original box; **front:** top view of the handle.

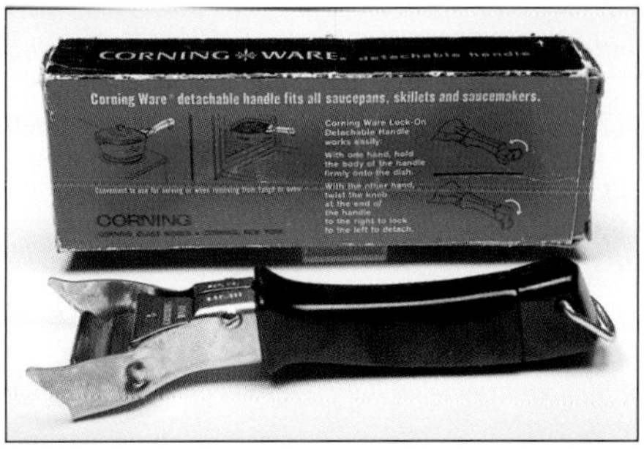

Detachable handle for saucepans, #P-10-HG, 7.5" long, metal with black plastic, end twists for putting on and off, ring on end, marked on the underside with: Corning Ware® Pat. No. 2,851,299, **$5.00 each. Back:** back view of box showing directions for use; **front:** underneath view of handle.

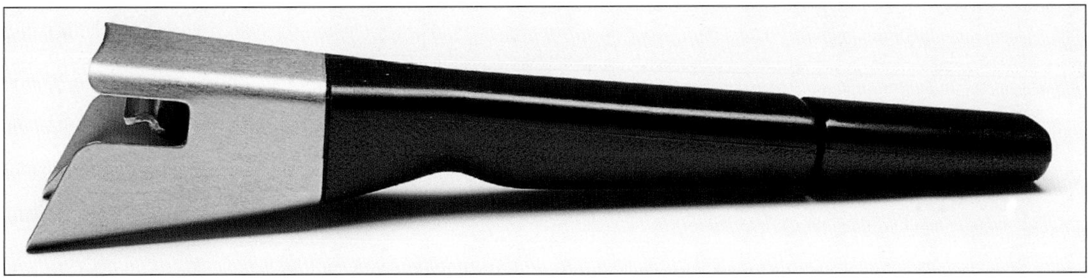

Detachable handle, A-10-11, 7.75" long, marked on underside of metal: Corning Ware® A-10-11, smooth top and stippled texture on the underside, **$5.00.**

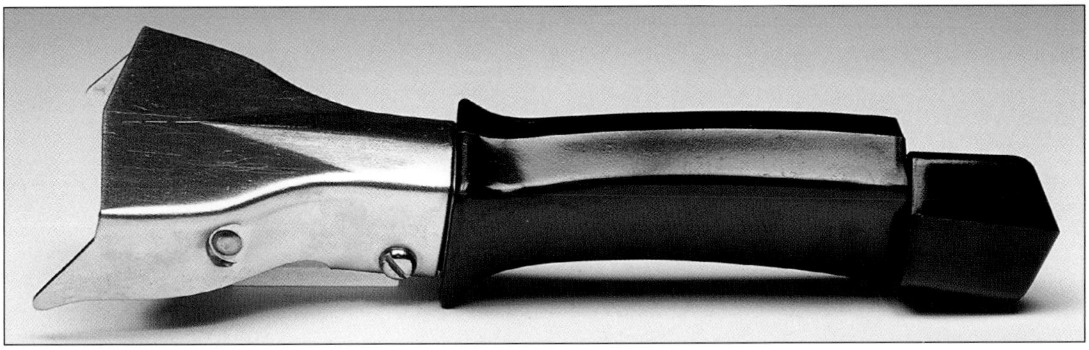

Detachable handle, 7.25" long, metal with black plastic, end twists for putting on and off, marked on the underside with: Corning Ware® Pat. No. 2,851,299 and No. 3,065,016, **$5.00.**

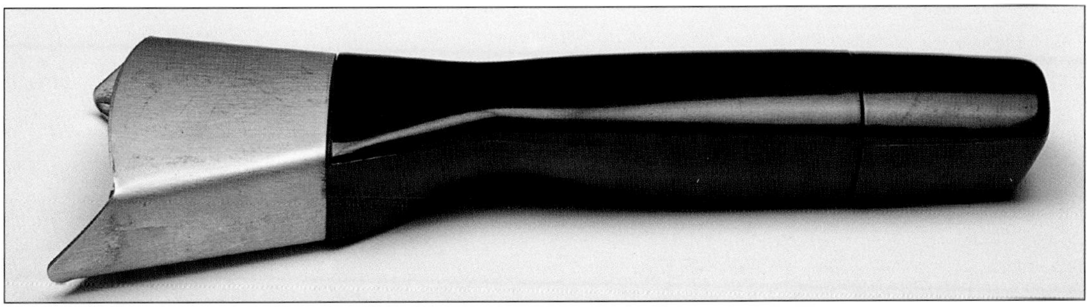

Detachable handle, 7.75" long, metal with black plastic, end twists for putting on and off, not marked, **$5.00.**

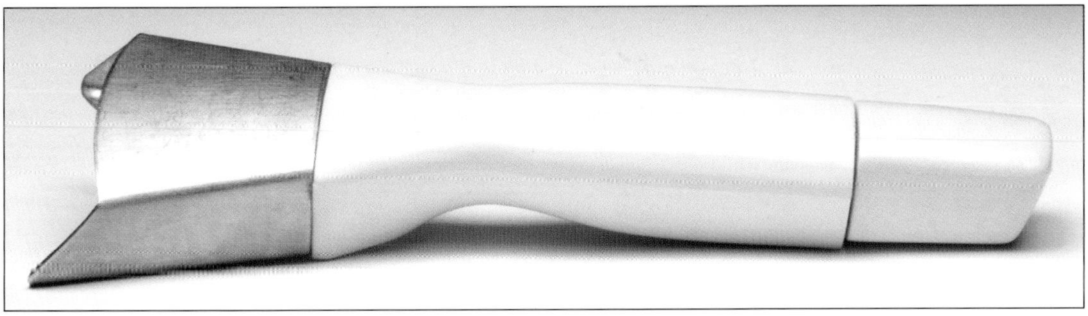

Detachable handle, 7.5" long, metal with white plastic, end twists for putting on and off, marked on the underside with: Corning Ware 2,851,299 and No. 5,025,016, **$10.00. Note:** This handle is very hard to find since it was only available for a short time.

A metal serving tray that Corning called a cradle was used to provide a way for placing the hot Corning pieces on the table. In addition, some had candle warmers in the base to also keep the food hot.

A nicely styled hot plate was made by another company for placing the hot Corning pieces on the table. They advertised using Corning cookware on their front box cover. In the center of the plastic framed hot plate was a piece of granite that would keep the food warm for an hour. You simply placed it the microwave for a couple of minutes to heat it up. The piece was then placed on the table with the Corning being set on top. It was a wonderful combination that wouldn't scratch or stain your Corning.

Go along item, Micro Hot Plate,1.5" tall, 8" wide, 10.25" long, white plastic with 5.75" wide granite center, hot plate for keeping food hot, **$8.50. Note:** Shown on the front is a floral Corning casserole.

World Kitchen

World Kitchen has actually been part of the house wares business for over 100 years but only recently under that name. Through the years many different purchases occurred that made this company into what it is today.

In 1888 a baking pan company was started by Edward Katzinger. This company was called Ekco®. In 1972 the new bake ware line called Baker's Secret® was introduced by Ekco®. Corning Glass Works purchased the Revere Ware® Corporation in 1988. The General Housewares Corporation bought Chicago Cutlery® in 1988. The Oxo Company was purchased by General Housewares in 1992. Borden Inc. purchased the Corning Consumer Products division in 1998. The following year, in 1999, Ekco® and General Housewares was purchased. This conglomerate of companies was renamed World Kitchen, Inc. in 2000. The company name was changed to World Kitchen, LLC in 2006.

Today, the household brands owned by this one company include: Baker's Secret®, Chicago Cutlery®, Corelle®, Corning Ware®, Ekco®, Magnalite®, Olfa®, Pyrex®, Revere Ware®, and Visions®.

Brochure of World Kitchen with Corning Ware® Corelle® Pyrex® Revere Chicago Cutlery and more.

French White, casserole, covered, #F-1 ½-B, 4.75" tall, 9.5" long, 7.5" wide, 1 ½ quart, oblong, glass lid, detail of bottom mark: microwave and oven safe Made in China 1 ½ qt. Corning Ware® French White® stoneware no stove top no broiler.

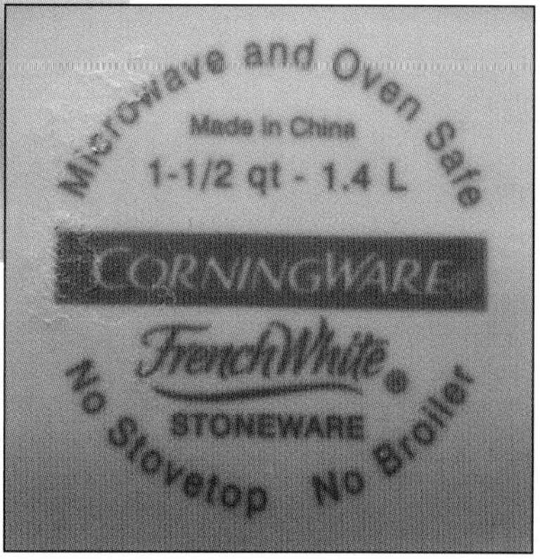

Detail of bottom mark: microwave and oven safe Made in China 1 ½ qt. Corning Ware® French White® stoneware no stove top no broiler.

After the purchase of the Corning Consumer Division in 1998, the Pyroceram® cookware products were eliminated. The new cookware was switched to be ceramic stoneware. Currently, the only cookware pattern still being made today is the French White. Various Corelle® dinnerware patterns are also being offered. Different types of accessory items are offered in many of the patterns.

Pyrex® glass lids are currently available in all sizes except for the petite pan. This small glass lid is extremely hard to find as a replacement on the secondary market. These new lids all have rayed centers. Plastic lids are available in all sizes. The new white plastic is very flexible and fit over the tab handles. This provides for a tight seal on any of the pans and makes for easier stacking in the cabinet.

Comparison of the new plastic lids showing the word, Corning Ware®. **Left:** 5.5" wide; **center:** 8.5" wide; **right:** 7.25" wide.

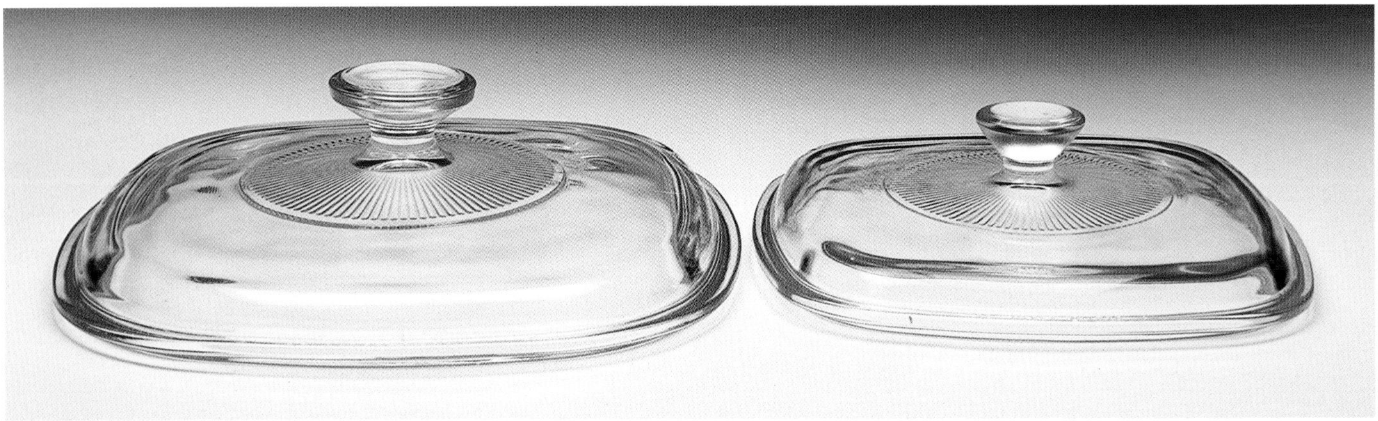

Comparison of the new glass lids with rayed centers. **Left**: 8.75″ wide, marked on edge: Pyrex® A 9 C; **right**: 7″ wide, marked on edge: Pyrex® A 7 C.

Special cleaning solutions can be purchased for keeping your cookware looking like new. World Kitchen has a paste material that will clean, polish, and protect your cookware. The formula for this is very similar to the original one offered by Corning. Bon Ami® is a powder cleanser that also will clean and polish. It is advertised as an earth friendly cleaner with no chlorine, perfume, or dye in the formula. It is listed as being recommended for Corning Ware® and Pyrex®. The nice thing about Bon Ami® is that it can be found at most grocery stores while the World Kitchen cleaner is only available in their own stores.

At many Outlet malls, there is a Corning Corelle® shop with a large assortment of the many brands they carry. Check on the World Kitchen web site, www.worldkitchen.com, to see if there is one near you. You will be amazed on the large assortment of kitchen related items that can be found there.

Left: Bon Ami™ cleanser; **center**: original Corning cleaner; **right**: World Kitchen cleaner

Replacements, Ltd.

Replacements, Ltd. located at 1089 Knox Road in Greensboro, North Carolina, is a great place to find many patterns. A huge staff is on hand to help you. Call them at 1-800-737-5223 or go on their web site at www.replacements.com to see if they carry your pattern. If they don't have it on hand, they will actively search for it and let you know when they have located it. If a pattern isn't normally handled, but they have numerous requests, they will make an attempt to have it in stock. Another valued service is the ability to identify a pattern for you. If you have some pieces and want more of them but don't know the name, you can email them a photo along with any markings and they will gladly see if they can be of help. They have a tremendous data base to do research.

Museums

There are two museums that furnished us archival material for this book. We encourage you to support them by becoming a member and enable them to continue acquiring material for research purposes and having wonderful displays for all of us to see.

Corning Museum of Glass One Museum Way, Corning, New York
Open daily 9am to 8pm
Membership: $35 individual or $60 dual family
Bi-annual newsletter; free admission, discount to events and publications
1-800-723-9156
www.cmog.org

West Virginia Museum of American Glass 230 Main Ave. Weston, West Virginia
Open daily noon to 5pm
Membership: $25
Quarterly magazine, free admission, discount to events and publications
1-304-269-5006
http://wmag.bglances.com

Bibliography

Books

Corning Glass Works. *The Corning Glass Center.* Corning, New York: Western Printing and Lithographing Co., 1958

Coroneos, Kyle. *The Complete Guide to Corning Ware and Visions Cookware*. Paducah, Kentucky: Collector Books, 2006

Dyer, Davis and Daniel Gross. *The Generations of Corning.* New York: Oxford University Press, 2001

Mauzy, Barbara. *Pyrex: The Unauthorized Collector's Guide.* Atglen, Pennsylvania: Schiffer Publishing, 2008

Rogove, Susan Tobier and Marcia Buan Steinhauer. *Pyrex by Corning: A Collector's Guide.* Marietta, Ohio: Antique Publications, 1993

Catalogs/Newsletters

American Ceramic Society. *American Ceramic Society Bulletin,* Westerfield, Ohio: American Ceramic Society, March 2000

Corning Incorporated, Inc. *Company Catalogs.* Corning, New York: Corning Glass, 1950s to 1990s

Corning Museum of Glass, *Archival material,* Corning, New York, Corning Museum of Glass, 1950s to 1990s.

Gaffer News, *Company newsletters.* Corning, New York: Corning Glass Works, 1950s to 1980s

West Virginia Museum of American Glass. *Archival material.* Weston, West Virginia: West Virginia Museum of American Glass, 1970s and 1980s.

Personal correspondence

Bardhan, Gail. Email and phone calls to author, Librarian at Corning Museum of Glass Rakow Library, 2008

Davis, Betty. Email to author, Corning Glass Archives Patent Department

Gable, Kristine. Email to author, Corning Glass Archives, 2008

Mecklenborg, Mark. Email to author, Staff Director at the American Glass Society, 2008

Six, Dean. Email and phone call to author, Researcher at Replacements, 2008

Stookey, Donald. Email to author, former Corning employee and inventor of Pyroceram®, 2008

Wilson, Jaime. Email to author, Customer Service at the American Glass Society, 2008

Wray, Peter. Email to author, Director of Communications at the American Glass Society, 2008

Web Sites

www.astro.caltech.edu/palomar/hale
www.ceramicbulletin.org
www.collectibles.about.com
www.corning.com
www.ebay.com
www.epinions.com
www.hubble.nasa.gov
www.recall-warnings.com
www.replacements.com
www.uspto.gov
www.worldkitchen.com